Wordsworth and the Composition of Knowledge

Studies in Nineteenth-Century British Literature

Regina Hewitt
General Editor

Vol. 15

PETER LANG
New York • Washington, D.C./Baltimore • Boston • Bern
Frankfurt am Main • Berlin • Brussels • Vienna • Oxford

Brad Sullivan

Wordsworth and the Composition of Knowledge

Refiguring Relationships Among Minds, Worlds, and Words

PETER LANG
New York • Washington, D.C./Baltimore • Boston • Bern
Frankfurt am Main • Berlin • Brussels • Vienna • Oxford

Library of Congress Cataloging-in-Publication Data

Sullivan, Brad.
Wordsworth and the composition of knowledge:
refiguring relationships among minds, worlds, and words / Brad Sullivan.
p. cm. — (Studies in nineteenth-century British literature; vol. 15)
Includes bibliographical references (p.) and index.
1. Wordsworth, William, 1770–1850—Philosophy. 2. Knowledge, Theory
of, in literature. 3. Philosophy in literature. I. Title. II. Series.
PR5892.P5 S85   821'.7—dc21   99-052472
ISBN 0-8204-4857-5
ISSN 1071-0124

Die Deutsche Bibliothek-CIP-Einheitsaufnahme

Sullivan, Brad:
Wordsworth and the composition of knowledge:
refiguring relationships among minds, worlds, and words / Brad Sullivan.
–New York; Washington, D.C./Baltimore; Boston; Bern;
Frankfurt am Main; Berlin; Brussels; Vienna; Oxford: Lang.
(Studies in nineteenth-century British literature; Vol. 15)
ISBN 0-8204-4857-5

The paper in this book meets the guidelines for permanence and durability
of the Committee on Production Guidelines for Book Longevity
of the Council of Library Resources.

© 2000 Peter Lang Publishing, Inc., New York

All rights reserved.
Reprint or reproduction, even partially, in all forms such as microfilm,
xerography, microfiche, microcard, and offset strictly prohibited.

Printed in the United States of America

For
Mom and Dad
Donna
Luke and Mariah

Contents

Acknowledgments	xi
List of Abbreviations	xiii
Introduction	1

Knowing Contexts   13

Chapter 1: Origins and Assumptions   15
- Origins of This Text   15
- Wordsworth's Original Purposes   19
- Assumptions: "Demonstrable Knowledge," Perception, and Moral Judgment   21
- My Critical Stance and Assumptions   23

Chapter 2: Enduring Knowledge Traditions   29
- Introduction   29
- Knowledge is Power   30
- Wordsworth the Poet, Coleridge the Philosopher-Critic: Our Cultural Predispositions at Work   32
- Plato's Bid for Knowledge-Power   37
- A Forgotten Voice   39
- Today's De(con)structive Model of Knowledge   42

Wordsworth's Critique of Systematic Knowing   49

Chapter 3: Exploring the Limits of Reason and Rational Systems   53
- The "Disenchantment" of Mechanical Philosophy   53
- The Problem of Reason   56
- Wordsworthian Connections and Relationships   61
- The Comprehensive Mind   66

Chapter 4: Constructing a Rhetorical Epistemology	**73**
Wordsworth's Principles of Knowing: Perception, Representation, and Considered Experience	77

Wordsworth's Alternative Model of Knowing — 83

Chapter 5: Perception and Participation	**87**
The Complexities of Perception	91
Two Worlds, Two Consciousnesses: Relationship-Centered Epistemology	92
Disciplining Perception	94
Chapter 6: Wordsworth's Ecology of Mind	**103**
Relating Perception, "Feeling" and Thinking	105
Emergent Patterns of Organization	107
Pleroma and Creatura: The *Difference* of Living Systems	109
Levels of Mental Process: We are Parts of Larger Minds	110
Systemic and Systematic Modes of Knowing: Calibration and Feedback	113
Chapter 7: Representation and Rhetoric	**117**
Wordsworth's Relations with Enlightenment "Rhetoric"	119
A Broader View of Rhetoric	121
The Classical Connection: Quintilian's *Institutes of Oratory*	123
Excursion: Reason and Habits of Mind	126
Habits of Mind and Education in Quintilian	129
The Power of Particular Experience and Context	133
Chapter 8: Poetry and Composing	**143**
Wordsworth's Rhetorical Stance	145
Wordsworth's View of "Poetry"	147
"Identification" and Burke's Broader View of Rhetoric	150
Poetic "Pleasure" as a Form of "Identification"	152
"We are Seven"	154
"Tintern Abbey"	157
"The Solitary Reaper"	163
Some Conclusions and New Directions	166

Contents

Postscript: Using Wordsworth's Model of Knowing   169

Notes   179

Works Cited   189

Index   195

Acknowledgments

This text should be considered as an experiment in critical discourse—an attempt both to discuss and embody an alternative model of knowing. My approach here might be considered "re-constructive," because I "take apart" several apparently distinct conceptual systems in order to begin putting them back together in new and integrated ways. I deconstruct some critical assumptions about language, knowledge, philosophy, rhetoric, and poetry, and by deconstructing them I aim to make possible a new synthesis that "reconstructs" the critical discourse about Wordsworth's work. I hope that the interdisciplinary methods I explore here prove to be as significant and helpful to my readers as the insights into Wordsworth that those methods offer in this particular case.

In his 1802 Preface to *Lyrical Ballads*, Wordsworth made the claim that "there is no knowledge without pleasure." And he acknowledged that the kind of pleasure he sought to advance and share was not simply sensual delight. In fact, he wrote, it encompassed suffering and pain. Wordsworth's "pleasure" is central to learning and growing. It is the delight of engaging in an activity that pushes us beyond ourselves and into a world of broader significance and meaning. It is the delight that sustains us through the pains and frustrations of practice so that we may experience the exhilaration of performing; it is the joy of sacrificing our egotistical interests in order to play a role in a larger system of harmony and meaning. That kind of pleasure has driven me to write and publish this book. I offer these ideas and explorations in the same spirit, hoping that they will spark similar pleasure in readers and move them to initiate further explorations.

Before proceeding, I want to thank the people who have served that role for me over the years. I believe that no significant advance in understanding is possible without the will to learn, a disciplined engagement of experience, the constructive friction of differing viewpoints and interpretations, and the long, patient work of synthesis. I thank Karen Chase-Levinson (Virginia) and Ann Fisher-Wirth (Mississippi), two of my greatest teachers, for inspiring me to learn, engaging me in the study of literature, and encouraging me to pursue graduate study and eventually join the ranks of university teachers. I thank Gregory Bateson, whom I consider a friend though I've never met him, for his efforts to bridge the Cartesian divides that haunt our culture, and for reminding his readers of the critical importance of perception in any model of knowing. I thank Morris Berman for his probing analysis of the impact of "scientific epistemology" on Western culture, and for introducing me to Gregory Bateson. I thank Linda Hanson and Paul Ranieri, my colleagues at Ball State University, who provided me with encouragement, guidance, and critical perspective throughout the process of writing this book. These two colleagues, in particular, helped me to work outside the "pre-established codes of decision" concerning Wordsworth, rhetoric, and literary criticism. I thank all my colleagues at Florida Gulf Coast University for their support as I tried to work on this project in the tiny cracks of time within our huge and exciting enterprise. In particular, I thank Rebecca Totaro, Ngure wa Mwachofi, Nora Demers, Mike McDonald, and Win Everham, who have sharpened my ideas with the delightful friction of interdisciplinary discussion.

Finally, and most importantly, I want to thank my family: my parents, David and Margaret Sullivan, for their ongoing support and love through the years; my children, Luke and Mariah, for helping me learn so much about joy, patience, and discipline along the way; and my wife and partner, Donna Beck, for sharing this most challenging process of knowing—and so many others—with me.

Abbreviations

References to Wordsworth's primary texts will employ the following system of abbreviation:

Borderers = Osborn's *The Borderers*

LWDW = de Selincourt and Shaver's *Letters of William and Dorothy Wordsworth: 1787-1805*

LWW = Hill's *Letters of William Wordsworth*

Pedlar = J. Wordsworth's *The Pedlar, Tintern Abbey, The Two-Part Prelude*

PoW = Hutchinson and de Selincourt's *Poetical Works*

PW = Owen and Smyser's *Prose Works*
   EoM = ["Essay on Morals"]
   Adv = 1798 Advertisement to *Lyrical Ballads*
   1800 Pref = 1800 Preface to *Lyrical Ballads*
   1802 Pref = 1802 Preface to *Lyrical Ballads*
   ES = 1815 "Essay Supplementary" to the Preface

Two-Part Prelude, 1805 Prelude, 1850 Prelude =
   J. Wordsworth, Abrams, and Gill's *The Prelude 1799, 1805, 1850*

Knowledge is not "discovered" or "delivered," despite the popular paradigms of science and higher education. Knowledge does not exist "out there" or "in here." Knowledge is a changing condition that emerges from and shapes our state of relationship and our mode of relating with others—creatures, ideas, views, and environments. We participate actively in the making of our own knowledge of the world. To deny this fact is to mislead ourselves into a view of objectivity that denies the value of personal experience, valorizes Truth and makes no room for Wisdom, excludes the affective and the physical from the domain of knowledge, and allows atrocities in the name of Reason. Yet we do deny it, and we risk our well-being as individuals and cultures by doing so. Our goal as learners and educators must be to reconnect "knowledge" in its broadest sense with the experiences, the feelings, and the needs of the individuals who construct and live within it. We must study and cultivate the complex recursive processes of knowing as well as bodies of knowledge. Wordsworth is one of the thinkers who can show us how.

Introduction

In this book, I enter two apparently divergent contemporary critical discussions of Wordsworth—discussions centering on the concepts of "ecology" and "rhetoric"—and suggest some ways in which the two can be productively related. The text explores a central epistemic problem that informs both of these contemporary discussions, offers a multilevel history of that problem and its effect on Western culture and literary criticism, and positions that problem at the heart of Wordsworth's poetic project. The problem, simply stated, is our uncritical acceptance and application of a Cartesian/Newtonian model of knowledge that can no longer be considered valid.

I

Our culture—and our critical discourse—have been built upon fundamentally Cartesian dichotomies: spirit/mind versus body/matter, individual mind versus social and natural worlds, feeling versus thinking. These dichotomies are at the foundations of our language; they form some of the most recalcitrant of what Wordsworth called our "pre-established codes of decision" ("Advertisement" to *Lyrical Ballads*). Even when a critical discourse explicitly questions them, they have a tendency to creep back into the text and to undermine efforts to escape them. The seriousness of this problem is embodied in the effort of David Bohm, a well-respected contemporary physicist, to create a "rheomode" of language that might help us to overcome the subject-verb-object orientation that limits our conceptions of the human/nature interface.[1] If we do not have a language that allows us to talk about relationships and interactions without dividing them into reified things and consciousnesses, then it is hard to conceive of them as primary characteristics of our world.

Contemporary scientists understand now the difficulty—and the essential falsehood—of dividing and subdividing the many processes of life into tidy and manageable categories. In physics, advances that illustrate that this difficulty is "built in" at the atomic level have been current since the early twentieth century. In biology and environmental studies, advances that clearly articulate the interdependence of living systems have emerged in the past few decades. But as Kroeber claims in *Ecological Literary Criticism*, scholars engaged in literary criticism have typically worked from the epistemic assumptions that guided nineteenth-century, rather than twentieth-century, science. These assumptions have created significant critical "blind spots" in the study of Wordsworth and British Romanticism. In spite of the many critical explorations of Wordsworth's philosophy (Grob, Rader), his reaction to science (Durrant, Stallknecht), and his views of the relation between the individual mind and the social and natural worlds (Clarke, Garber, Jones, and Rzepka)—subjects that encourage an investigation of Wordsworth's epistemology—no one has explored the possibility that his writings might represent an epistemic experiment in which poetry plays a key role.[2]

The history of Wordsworth criticism shows that efforts to read his writing within the framework of Cartesian oppositions inevitably make his thinking seem obtuse, paradoxical, and even naive. If we assume that Wordsworth offered a doctrine of personal experience that was meant to *replace* science and technology—even "objective" thinking—then it becomes nearly impossible to take his thinking seriously. Matthew Arnold took this position, insisting that we should celebrate the personal power of Wordsworth's poetry and simply dismiss his rather muddle-headed philosophy from consideration.[3]

While no one reads Wordsworth from the Arnoldian position today, my point is that Wordsworth has been read, and continues to be read, through what might be called a "Cartesian filter." And as a result, his complicated statements in the Prefaces concerning the connections between thinking and feeling, mind and "Nature," and body and spirit have been either (1) ignored completely or (2) oversimplified by being recast in dualistic terms. Critics who analyze them typically "murder to dissect" by demanding that Wordsworth's thinking conform to their own assumptions. They strive to make them falsely clear rather than richly complicated.

In order to illustrate the unfortunate implications of reading Wordsworth through a "Cartesian filter," I will briefly examine some important positions taken in Wordsworthian scholarship and show how

Cartesian assumptions have repeatedly shaped our readings of Wordsworth. We must begin, of course, with M. H. Abrams' account of Wordsworth's "literary theory" in his milestone book *The Mirror and the Lamp*. In this book, Abrams claimed that the 1800 Preface to *Lyrical Ballads* had "something of the aspect of a romantic manifesto" (100), and effectively established that Wordsworth's writings were central to the development of romantic theories of poetry and literature in England. As a result, this text has served as a point of departure for, and has set the terms of, much subsequent scholarship. Unfortunately, Abrams relied on Cartesian oppositions when reading Wordsworth, reducing many of the complexities of the Preface to simple dichotomies. For example, he began from the premise that for Wordsworth (and later romantics) "Poetry is the expression or overflow of feeling, or emerges from a process of imagination in which feelings play the crucial part" (101). His assumption was that "feeling" could only be seen as a category opposed to "thinking." He neglected to examine the difficulties of interpreting just what Wordsworth meant by "feeling," a term that Wordsworth sometimes used in the Preface to indicate "sensation" or "perception" as well as "emotion." And he did not attempt to enter into the complexities of Wordsworth's discussion of how "feeling" and "thinking" are related—complexities that qualify Wordsworth's now famous statement that "poetry is the spontaneous overflow of powerful feelings."

Starting from this assumption, Abrams articulated further "propositions about the nature and criteria of poetry" (100–01) that Wordsworth supposedly set forth and his contemporaries adopted. He framed Wordsworth's opposition between the language of Poetry and the language of Science in terms established by late Romantic and early Victorian critics—"the difference between expression and description, or between emotive language and cognitive language" (101). He even went so far as to quote an 1835 source that carried this distinction to its far extreme: "'Prose is the language of *intelligence*, poetry of *emotion*'" (101). By this time, Abrams was already far removed from Wordsworth's complex and thoughtful struggle to articulate a different view of poetry in the Preface, and he was able to state the nature of Wordsworth's contribution in terms that seem straightforward but are really far too simplistic:

> Wordsworth, then, the first great romantic poet, may also be accounted the critic

whose highly influential writings, by making the feelings of the poet the center of critical reference, mark a turning point in English literary theory. (103)

Typical of critics working in the Cartesian mode, Abrams sought clarity by reducing the difficulties of Wordsworth's Prefaces to a workable formula. And by offering a framework built on simple dichotomies, he has contributed to the field of pervasive assumptions about Wordsworth that began with Coleridge, came down to us through Arnold, and has informed Wordsworth scholarship ever since. Two of the most powerful assumptions that Abrams crystallized are:

1. Wordsworth developed an "expressive" discursive stance centered on his own utterances and feelings rather than on any substantial rhetorical engagement of subjects or audiences, and
2. Wordsworth was more concerned with issues of "feeling" than with issues of thinking, and he set a course for poetry that followed this path.

Both of these assumptions are framed by Cartesian dichotomies between "mind" and "world" and between "feeling" and "thinking"—dichotomies that Wordsworth confronts directly and vehemently in the evolving Preface to *Lyrical Ballads*.

These two assumptions have made it very hard to deal with Wordsworth's self-proclaimed moral and social purposes—his clearly stated urgency to make a difference for his culture—and his "philosophy." How can a man who centers his work on his own feelings and expressions be effective at changing anything? And how can a romantic poet, whose focus is feelings, be an effective thinker and philosopher? Many critics have been aware of and have stressed the fact that Wordsworth was attempting to rescue poetry from its own artificiality and to bring it back to terms with "real life" (Sharrock, for example). But they have found his philosophy inconsistent (if not incoherent) in dualistic terms, and they have found it difficult to examine his social and moral purposes within the domain of his seemingly subjective and expressive stance.

A frustrating example is Robert Langbaum's *The Poetry of Experience*. In this text, Langbaum implied that for Wordsworth, and for "romantic" poets, knowledge was an ongoing process that started with and was sustained by individual perception and personal experience.

These individuals, he claimed, worked from the conviction that

> formulation itself must never be allowed to settle into dogma, but must emerge anew every day out of experience. It must be lived, which is to say that it must carry within it its subjective origin, its origin in experience and self-realization. (20)

In passages like this one, Langbaum came about as close as any other scholar to the core of Wordsworth's epistemology. Langbaum's statement that formulation (conceptual knowledge) must "be lived" and must always emerge from "its subjective origin" led him to the brink of a significantly different approach to Wordsworth's views of knowing—an approach that would have entered into the complex continuums between subjectivity and objectivity, between feeling and thinking, and between individual minds and the worlds that they attempt to "formulate."

But Langbaum read Wordsworth with Cartesian assumptions, and as a result his analysis could not take such a direction. He claimed that romanticism was "a doctrine of experience, an attempt to salvage on science's own empiric grounds the validity of individual perception against scientific abstractions" (27). The key word here is "against"—as if somehow we could throw out all of what scientific abstractions have offered and replace them by a doctrine of purely personal experience. And that, of course, is both impossible and undesirable. By cleaving the world into the "individual" and the "scientific," Langbaum again placed Wordsworth and romantic poets at large in the camp of "subjectivity," implying that their "doctrine of experience" could have no real import beyond the perceptual world of a few poets (and critics).

In the contemporary discussions of Wordsworth, this problem remains. New Historical readings of Wordsworth again assert his tendency to secure "subjective" retreats by overlooking or obfuscating the history of his times. Even efforts to take Wordsworth's poetic project seriously—to see it as socially-engaged—often fail because of the "Cartesian trap." For example, in *The Supplement of Reading*, Rajan claims that the Preface to *Lyrical Ballads*

> Enlists poetics in the service of hermeneutics by arguing that poetry can facilitate understanding across social boundaries. (136)

Here we see a desire to envision poetry as a tool for cultural intervention—and a clear sense that Wordsworth saw it that way. But then, in the very next sentence, Descartes intervenes:

> More specifically, it [the Preface] expands hermeneutics in a social direction by making the sharing of feelings the foundation for the establishment of transcultural values. (136)

Like Abrams, Rajan employs "feelings" without explaining just what Wordsworth meant by the word, and does not explain just how interpretation and feeling might be connected. She goes on to state that what the *Lyrical Ballads* share "is an insistence on private feeling as a value in itself" and to conclude that the "impulse behind the collection is thus the naturalizing of a poetics of subjectivity: a poetics that would otherwise seem a romantic imposition on a world already encroached upon by the new discourses later developed by thinkers like Marx" (139). And so we return to a poetry based on "feeling": a "poetics of subjectivity." And no matter how much we try to take such a position seriously, we have a hard time seeing such a poetics as a serious contribution to our Western discourse of knowledge. In the words of Kroeber, "we cannot conceive a poet being so confident of the intellectual and practical worth of a mere poem" (17). Cartesian assumptions continue to rule us.

But in contemporary discussions of Wordsworth, we also have the arguments of Bate, Kroeber, and Hewitt.[4] And they offer new approaches to Wordsworth that are very promising. They take issue with the limitations imposed by critics who presuppose that Wordsworth is, above all else, "subjective," and begin to frame ways in which we can see the seriousness of Wordsworth's poetic project and—perhaps—even use Wordsworth's ideas today. I wish to extend their efforts by looking back to the sources of the problem that has plagued both our culture and the critical discourse about Wordsworth: to show that what Bate and Kroeber call "cold war criticism" emerged from a philosophical tradition that has its roots in ancient Greece.

In this text, I propose that Wordsworth's writings represent a carefully considered and disciplined effort to recast or replace the Cartesian/Newtonian model of knowing. I show that by exploring the ways Wordsworth attempted to subvert and remake Cartesian assumptions, we can enter a frame of reference in which personal identity, social structures, and the natural world are all interrelated rather than exclusive of each other. And we can begin to "see Wordsworth whole" without reducing the multiplicity of his work to a few simple rules.

I am not the first to attempt an extended non-Cartesian reading of Wordsworth. John Rudy's *Wordsworth and the Zen Mind* nicely illustrates the critical shortcomings of approaching Wordsworth with Cartesian assumptions, and very effectively moves discussion of Wordsworth outside the bounds of Cartesian dualism.[5] The "idiom of Zen" provides him with a different paradigm for examining Wordsworth's compositions, and his account captures the movement away from simple oppositions in Wordsworth's thinking. But Rudy overstates his case when he claims that

> Much of Wordsworth's poetry ... labors to hide or to obliterate the felt presence of a separate organizing or opposing self in favor of a prejudgmental, prereflective consciousness so deeply aligned with a perceived matrix of creative forces that it is impossible to say where the world's energies leave off and those of the poet begin. (12)

This claim simply cannot account for some of the central tendencies in Wordsworth's work: his careful attention to the development of personal identity, his continual effort to revise and re-think his work (and himself) so well-documented by scholars like Leader and Johnson, his struggle in poems like "Tintern Abbey" and the "Immortality Ode" with the sense of being "two consciousnesses," each of which offers something of value, and his insistence on a "purpose" for poetry. It is revealing that Rudy's index does not contain an entry for the word "purpose"—a word that Wordsworth uses pointedly to focus his poetic project in the Prefaces.

Like Rudy, I utilize a different paradigm to recontextualize Wordsworth's poetic project in non-Cartesian terms. But I ground my project in what Wordsworth would have known—the language and concepts of classical rhetoric that were at his disposal—and attempt to show how Wordsworth sought to extend rhetorical thinking into the domain of what he called "the language of the sense." In order to achieve this goal I offer some extended discussion of some lesser-known principles of Quintilian—which include, interestingly enough, the importance of meditation in the act of composing—and integrate some of the seminal ideas of twentieth-century scientists—particularly Gregory Bateson, who instigated cybernetic and systemic inquiries in the fields of biology, psychology, anthropology, and communications[6], and Antonio Damasio, a neurologist who has illustrated the necessary connection between "emotion" and "reason" and offered a non-reductive way to link physical and mental processes into a continuum[7]—to show that Wordsworth's efforts to establish connections between mind and body, mind and world, and feeling and thinking were coherent and powerful rather than "muddleheaded" or simply "paradoxical."[8] The rhetorical tradition articulates the interrelationships that Wordsworth explored: between language and the world being represented, between speaker and audience, between feeling and thinking, and between thinking and acting. As I state in my postscript, a revitalization of rhetoric can complement the "systems thinking" that has become predominant in contemporary science—particularly biology and ecology—and perhaps offer a much-needed and meaningful new role for the study of literature and composition. I hope that others will pursue the connections that I suggest in this book.

II

In the 1790s Wordsworth was setting out to do more than simply rescue poetry, though that is undoubtedly part of what he sought to do. As an author, he entered a culture that was putting the final touches on a model of knowledge that treated "reality" as an ontological category and "language" and "perception" as epistemological categories. Language could be used to represent reality, or to distort the perception of reality, but it had no impact on reality itself (because, in Locke's formulation, the essential forms of reality existed prior to both perception and language).[9] Knowledge had been claimed by the scientists and philosophers, who asserted that they used language transparently to convey reality. Orators and poets were left with an uncertain role in the culture, because their discourse could make no such claim.

In general terms, the discourses of philosophy and science had attained the status of knowledge because they purported to deal with fact and logic and truth in clear, non-affective language. "Rhetoric" was seen as a discourse of persuasion, "interest," and "enthusiasm"—highly loaded terms of the time—which might generate revolution but which had nothing to do with knowledge. And "Poetry" had been placed in the role of speaking the truths of science and philosophy with the grace and beauty of art. This division between the discourse of knowledge and the discourse of art is stated elegantly in Alexander Pope's much-repeated dictum:

> *True Wit* is *Nature* to Advantage drest,
> What oft was *Thought*, but ne'er so well *Exprest*.[10]

This division, of course, placed poetry in a separate category from knowledge and threatened to trivialize the poetic use of language.

But despite the growing confidence in Newtonian science and its explanation of the world as "matter in motion," difficult questions about the nature and limits of human knowing were in the air. What was the source of authoritative knowledge? Edmund Burke's *Reflections on the Revolution in France* deals with this question, and in fact can be seen as a treatise on "cultural epistemology" as well as on politics.[11] If moral philosophy cannot produce working systems for understanding and effecting human behavior, where will human behavior go? (Framed by the French Revolution, this question was indeed terrifying!) If science does not deal with issues of value and affect, what will? What are the technical or instrumental limits on human knowing? And is it worthwhile to philosophize about them (one of Hume's final questions)?

By the late eighteenth century, the answers to these questions that had been—and were being—offered were cementing into place a scientific epistemology like the one described by Morris Berman in *The Reenchantment of the World*. That epistemology was technology-centered, emerging from the belief that "mind" and "spirit" were "internal" features of human beings, and that the world (including the human body) was "external," consisting of "matter in motion" to be shaped and used as humans saw fit. In effect, the faculty of reason had gradually been reduced from Right Reason, which was a faculty capable of judging morality as well as veracity, to instrumental reason, which was seen simply as a tool for building both systems of thought and new industries.[12] In this epistemology, "to know something is to control it" (Berman 40). Issues of personal value and meaning were not being clearly addressed, except perhaps in limited utilitarian and capitalistic terms.

Berman claims that this epistemology represents nothing short of a cultural madness—the purposeful dismissal of entire dimensions of human experience and knowing in the name of utility and a myth of objective knowledge. My claim is that Wordsworth enters the scene at just the right time to sense this development clearly enough to battle it, but that he lacks the critical vocabulary to articulate it fully and the support to beat it. His repeated references in his Prefaces and letters to the problems of his culture should have a direct bearing on the way we approach his work. In fact, he was trying desperately to rescue his culture from a killing epistemology—one that, by implying that matters of fact (seen as "objective knowledge") can and should be separated from matters of value (seen as "subjective" or "personal" choices), has brought us to the brink of destruction in the twentieth century.

His tools for grappling with this underlying cultural problem were primitive in some ways—partly drawn from, and limited by, what Abrams calls "an amalgam" of "eighteenth-century speculations" and "prevalent ideas" (104). But as a student of classical rhetoric, and a participant in the broader processes of the natural world he grew up in, he was better equipped than we might think to respond intelligently to the epistemic problems of his day and age. This text attempts to step outside the confines of the killing epistemology that he sought to balance and correct, and to place the central terms and patterns of his work within a broader context framed by the ancient and ongoing battle between philosophy and rhetoric on one hand and an alternative epistemological stance—an "ecology of mind" offered by Gregory Bateson in our own century—on the other. Employing his knowledge of classical rhetoric, particularly Quintilian's *Institutes of Oratory*, and his own developing sense of the complexities of perception and representation, Wordsworth developed an epistemological stance that was founded on personal experience, representation, relationship, and revision rather than on the establishment of "demonstrable" or "objective" knowledge. He centered his epistemology on what he perceived to be a continuum connecting perception, feeling, thinking and acting, and on the integrative relationship between individual minds and what he saw as larger mindlike processes (particularly "Nature").

What this means, of course, is that Wordsworth chose to view epistemology in terms of "composition" rather than in terms of "correctness" or "error." The title of this text—*Wordsworth and the Composition of Knowledge*—comes from his convictions that human meaning and value are composed by mental processes and representations and that knowing is a state of relationship rather than an accumulation of data. He seeks to return poetry to its origins, not in "primitive utterance of feelings" but in "poesis" or making. He views knowing as an ongoing process of representing experience both biologically, in perception, and intellectually, in mental models. Perception—what he calls the "language of the sense"—and language itself are both processes of representation. The aim of knowing cannot be to ascertain a final, absolute "Truth" or to attain a "correct" representation of an "external" reality. Instead, the aim of knowing is to tune and develop both perception and cognition in such a way as to develop good habits of thought and action. Knowing should not be limited to individual perceptions, to cultural traditions and prevailing opinions, or to a mystical "oneness with the world." It should be a dynamic engagement of all three. And language, when used appropriately, can help initiate and sustain that engagement rather than closing it by asserting the final validity of mental models or systems of thinking.

Wordsworth frames his views of poetry and the poet in these terms, recognizing that composition embodying real events and feelings can become part of the field of experience for a reader who engages it. As a result, we can both compose experience in life and experience composition in poetry. And knowing in both cases is always artful, charged with creative possibilities and with the moral imperative not to misuse them.

Wordsworth's interest in travel, his recurrent use of borderers (social outcasts and misfits) as the subjects of his early poetry, and his effort to engage readers with "the real language of men in a state of vivid sensation" (*1802 Pref, PW* 1: 119) all spring from this epistemology. He recognized that we tend to approach new experiences with a firm set of "pre-established codes of decision" (*Adv, PW* 1: 106) and that those mental models can trap us. Yet he also believed that our habits of perception, thought, and action could be improved by way of new experiences. This text argues that the keys for him were engagement and participation, which were both initiated and sustained by what he calls "pleasure" in the Preface. As he writes in the Preface, "we have no knowledge ... but what has been built up by pleasure, and exists in us by pleasure alone" (*Pref, PW* 1: 140). Learning can only take place when the individual opens him or herself to new experiences. And that openness may not be purposive in rational terms, which tend to reduce new experiences to what we aim to get out of them. Excursions, encounters with unfamiliar viewpoints, and surprising moments can be a source of significant learning—if approached with the right state of mind. Wordsworth's rhetorical task was to create that state of mind in himself and in his readers.

This text makes no attempt to complete or close the discussions of Wordsworth that it opens. Instead it seeks to provide a helpful context and useful critical tools for further inquiry. By articulating the representation-based model of knowing that informs Wordsworth's discourse experiments, and grounding it in his obviously powerful personal engagement with the natural world and the rhetorical tradition that formed the center of his education, I aim to provide a starting point for more fruitful discussions of his literary theory, his philosophy, his educational ideas, his social and moral purposes, and his poetic and rhetorical strategies for reaching an audience. And within the broader context provided by Berman, I also suggest that Wordsworth's insights are worth considering as we reshape academic and cultural views of knowing in our own day and age.

Knowing Contexts

Chapter 1
Origins and Assumptions

Origins of This Text

> We take a handful of sand from the endless landscape of awareness around us and call that handful of sand the world... it's necessary to see that part of that landscape, inseparable from it, which must be understood, is a figure in the middle of it, sorting sand into piles. To see the landscape without seeing this figure is not to see the landscape at all.
> —Robert Pirsig, *Zen and the Art of Motorcycle Maintenance*

As a student taking my first graduate class in Romantic poetry, I found William Wordsworth very appealing on an intuitive level. His better compositions seemed to offer wisdom; I felt they embodied significant and valuable insights about the human mind and the world. I read and re-read his work, and found it more and more compelling. Yet even with a rigorous training in literature and critical thinking, I could not comfortably reason my way through his theories and his modes of experimentation with language and poetic form. His definitions of poetry and the poet's role created logical difficulties and contradictions; he used terms in ways that indicated they should bear meanings that they could not support fully or well; he made passionate claims concerning social and moral purposes that remained ill-defined in his texts. I felt that the accounts I read of his theory and his poetry were wrong in a very important way, but I couldn't put my finger on it. I didn't know enough yet.

I took a course in classical rhetoric the following year, and spent a considerable amount of time reading and questioning the texts of Isocrates, Plato, Aristotle, Cicero, and Quintilian. As I read Isocrates and Quintilian in particular, I discovered many points of resonance with Wordsworth's positions on discourse and knowledge and education. Isocrates' *Against the Sophists* and Book 10 of Quintilian's *Institutes of Oratory*, in particular, stressed that knowing, speaking, and acting formed a living continuum. They, like Wordsworth, sensed that symbolic representation, literary creation, transmission of knowledge, and moral action are interconnected and emergent facets of the mind's engagement with experience.

I began to catalog the connections between Quintilian's worldview and Wordsworth's. Both insist that to attempt to argue an audience into belief is less important than *moving* them by way of passionate engagement. Both stress a central reference point for human discourse and action called "Nature." Both offer a vision of education in which long experience and practice leads to facility of expression and wisdom and moral action. When I discovered a reference to Quintilian in Wordsworth's early letters, I was delighted. The more I read, the more seriously I took these connections.

But I was not interested in simply analyzing literary or intellectual connections. To do a source study that traced Wordsworth's indebtedness to Quintilian's ideas would not have done justice to the exciting way that Wordsworth used those ideas in his work. Instead, I began to see further possibilities for exploration. And as I pursued them, and made further connections, I began to have a much broader view of Wordsworth's poetic efforts. As I re-read and re-considered Wordsworth's Prefaces, the *Lyrical Ballads*, and *The Prelude*, I began to see them in the context of an ongoing battle concerning the nature of valid knowledge.

Isocrates and Plato offered distinctly different models of valid knowledge in ancient Athens. Isocrates insisted that we could have no universal truth, that our knowing should continually emerge from and shape our practices, that speaking and knowing were intimately connected, and that our aim should always be right action within our immediate context. Plato insisted that universal Truth was present, even if not fully accessible, that knowing should emerge from study in the form of questioning and reasoning, that speaking was only connected to knowing when it was bound by the rules of dialectic, and that our aim should always be to find the Truth and then to apply it to any and all contexts. Aristotle then made the powerful, and dangerous, maneuver of fusing the Platonic insistence on demonstrable knowledge with a firm grounding in sensory experience. By doing so, he laid the groundwork for both the aims and the methods of Enlightenment empirical philosophy and science. This is a highly simplified sketch of a complex development of ideas, but in outline it holds true.[1]

Wordsworth wrote at a time in which Enlightenment views of

knowledge were rapidly becoming assumptions rather than debatable ideas. Who could question the validity and power of Newton's great system? Who could question the vast force of scientific inquiry? Few would. But Wordsworth sensed that knowing was more than deduction and induction, more than the cataloguing of facts and figures, more than predictive power. And in his early compositions, he carried out an ongoing exploration of, and response to, the dangers of treating systematic, scientific knowledge as if it were the only form of valid knowledge. His work is not a reaction against science, but an attempt to complete science by broadening and deepening his—and his audience's—sense of what it is "to know."

Our views of knowledge, like the Enlightenment views that Wordsworth faced, have been established within and limited by Platonic/ Aristotelian philosophy and Cartesian/Newtonian science. Wordsworth criticism has been written within this framework, so his work has usually been viewed using hierarchical, linear, and systematic terms of knowledge. This framework has also made it very easy to consider Wordsworth's rejection of systematic thinking and writing to be a weakness rather than a carefully made discursive choice. It encourages us to assume that Wordsworth rejected systematic thinking because either he could not think systematically (he was by nature an inconsistent, and therefore less valuable, thinker) or he wouldn't think systematically because he was not willing to do the hard work of clarifying and systematizing his theory.

In fact, however, Wordsworth's rejection of systematic, linear thinking was quite thoughtful and well informed. It began as early as the fragmentary "Essay on Morals" (1798), and it was developed and sustained within the mandates of a coherent and powerful intellectual tradition: a tradition that originated in ancient Greece with the Sophists and that has remained an important intellectual undercurrent ever since. This tradition, which I will call "rhetorical" to differentiate it from "philosophical," though there is no simple opposition between them, provides a more coherent point of entry into Wordsworth's work.

What I am calling the rhetorical tradition requires some elucidation and expansion. In general terms, I am referring to the tradition of thinking that considers situations or particular contexts—what the Sophists would have called "kairos"—to be inextricable from processes of knowing and acting. This tradition stresses the processes of knowing as well as the products, resists the idea of universal truths, asserts that good judgment and action are more important than abstract principles, and considers all systems in the light of broader systemic contexts. One of my assumptions is that the Sophists' insistence that meaning and value were always negotiated within multiple contexts is not far removed from contemporary ecological claims that ecosystems must be understood within the broader systems (contexts) that encompass them. In both, negotiation and composition and context are central, rather than final meanings and truths. They require ongoing re-examination and a sense of humility.

This text considers, within the context provided by both the classical rhetorical tradition and twentieth century efforts to revise science, Wordsworth's attempt to develop a model of knowing that re-admits the affective, personal, context-bound elements of knowing. It reads Wordsworth's rejection of eighteenth-century poetics in his early compositions as part of an ongoing attempt to reconstruct rhetoric in epistemic, rather than ornamental, terms. These early texts, including the "Essay on Morals," the *Lyrical Ballads* (and all the Prefaces), the 1797 *Borderers*, and the 1805 *Prelude*, do much more than sketch out a new direction for poetry. In fact, they establish a broad rhetorical approach to knowing that is constructed in terms of relationship, interaction, and negotiation rather than in terms of traditional dichotomies such as subject and object, mind and thing, art and science, and so on. Within this rhetorical framework, Wordsworth defines poetry and the poet's role in terms of process and ongoing interaction of the developing "self" with developing social and natural contexts.

The early texts have been chosen because they represent Wordsworth's point of departure and because the scope of this text does not allow a complete survey of Wordsworth's career. My study is completely consistent with Leader's account of Wordsworth's effort to refine his poetry through revision. The epistemic model that I sketch out here would have made Wordsworth an inveterate reviser, and the patterns that I find in the early texts are refined and extended in the later texts. I will make comparative references to the 1850 *Prelude* from time to time to show how this is so.

Wordsworth's Original Purposes

to treat the subject [of Poetry and the theory on which my poems are written] with the clearness and coherence, of which I believe it to be susceptible, it would be necessary to give a full account of the present state of the public taste in this country, and to determine how far this taste is healthy or depraved; which, again, could not be determined, without pointing out in what manner language and the human mind act and re-act on each other, and without tracing the revolutions, not of literature alone, but likewise of society itself. (1800 Pref, PW 1: 121)

if the object which I have proposed to myself were genuinely attained, a species of poetry would be produced, which is genuine poetry; in its nature well adapted to interest mankind permanently, and likewise important in the multiplicity and quality of its moral relations. (1800 Pref, PW 1: 158)

Poetry is the breath and finer spirit of all knowledge; it is the impassioned expression which is in the countenance of all Science ... the Poet binds together by passion and knowledge the vast empire of human society, as it is spread over the whole earth, and over all time. (1802 Pref, PW 1: 141)

In his Prefaces and letters, William Wordsworth claims more for himself as a poet, and for poetry as an activity of mind, than was ever claimed by eighteenth-century poets. He claims that his subject matter as a poet is "every subject which can interest the human mind" (*Adv, PW* 1: 116) and that poetry is "the breath and finer spirit of all knowledge" (*1802 Pref, PW* 1: 141). In the 1802 Preface, he relates poetry and science in some very interesting ways, never claiming that poetry is science, yet insisting that it is a valuable and critically important domain of human knowing and action. He explicitly connects poetry with moral knowledge, with individual perception, and with social purpose throughout his Prefaces. And he hopes to create a "class of Poetry ... well adapted to interest mankind permanently, and not unimportant in the multiplicity and in the quality of its moral relations" (*1800 Pref, PW* 1: 120).

But ever since Wordsworth's own times, critics have had a hard time understanding or accepting Wordsworth's broad claims for poetry. In the culture of science and high technology, such claims sound like prophetic claptrap, like "divine wind" rather than substantial ideas. In the view of our knowledge establishment, only methods and results that can claim to be scientific are accepted as knowledge. Poetry can make no such claim, and thus cannot be a significant discourse of knowledge. As a result, we tend to humor Wordsworth's claims as Matthew Arnold did, rather than paying them much serious attention.

Unfortunately, such critics seem to have lost touch with a broad knowledge tradition that runs all the way back to ancient Greece—the tradition of classical rhetoric in which the knowing required for moral judgment and pragmatic action, rather than the knowing of "demonstrable truth," was the central issue. They have become so firmly entrenched in the Platonic/Aristotelian philosophical framework that they cannot effectively recognize or use the broader tradition within which philosophy grew. Wordsworth explicitly connects himself with this broad knowledge tradition in the 1815 "Essay Supplementary to the Preface" when he writes "her [poetry's] privilege and her *duty*, is to treat of things not as they *are*, but as they *appear*; not as they exist in themselves, but as they *seem* to exist to the *senses*, and to the *passions*" (*ES, PW* 2: 410). Here, Wordsworth is about as specific as he can be about taking what Aristotle considered the domain of *doxa*—rhetorical knowledge—as the domain of poetry.[2] And Wordsworth does not accept the prevailing idea (after Plato/Aristotle and even today) that such knowledge is less valuable or real or important than demonstrable or philosophical knowledge.

Wordsworth did not see poetry as the handmaiden of science. He had no desire to delight a handful of literati by dressing prevailing knowledge in delightful figures and flowing rhythms. Instead, he offered poetry as a vital and living counterpart of science, as a discourse of knowledge accessible to all human beings. He sketched out a relationship between poetry and science not unlike the relationship that Aristotle suggested between rhetoric and dialectic.[3] Wordsworth asserts that science, much like Aristotle's dialectic, deals with demonstrable knowledge—with the impersonal, abstract reasonings of mathematics and logic. Poetry, like Aristotle's rhetoric, deals with the domain of what seems to be—with the personal, particular struggles to find and make meaning within the individual and social contexts of daily life. But for Wordsworth, that distinction placed poetry, not science, in the position of greatest importance for human knowing.

Wordsworth sought to be a thinker and a teacher. Yet we tend to engage his work as if he were merely a poet who was out of his depth when he attempted to "do philosophy." Hewitt's claim that the multiplicity of Wordsworth's poetic forms can be attributed to his efforts to reach a shifting, uncertain audience[4]—that their very variety provides evidence of a coherent process—can also be applied to Wordsworth's thinking in general. The inconsistencies in his philosophy emerge from two things: (1) his sense that mental process—and human experience—is too complicated and rich to be contained by any systematic, hierarchical model of knowing, and (2) his resulting refusal of rigid systematic thinking in favor of a more flexible experience-based approach to knowing. He grapples with huge questions—questions that are still largely unresolved—and he tries to express both the questions and his tentative answers in a late eighteenth-century language that was ill suited to the task. His answers center on the primary importance of *perception*, or the "language of the sense" ("Tintern Abbey," *PoW* 165), and *rhetoric*, broadly construed as symbolic construction of meaning. Instead of positing a domain of "pure knowledge," free of the difficulties of interpretation and opinion, Wordsworth's model attempts to reconstruct and validate the world of doxa. His aim is to reground knowledge in personal experience and opinion—not "idle opinion" (as opposed to "demonstrable knowledge") but educated opinion emerging from and shaping experience.

Assumptions: "Demonstrable Knowledge," Perception, and Moral Judgment

Philosophers have always had to confront the troublesome way in which the domain of doxa—opinions, personal viewpoints, particular contexts, and what "seems to be true" in those contexts—mediates and complicates our efforts to know any lasting "truth." To accept that we cannot know truth and must act on the basis of each new situation as it arises is to give up any hope for learning and progress and lasting values. Yet to assert that truth can be known, catalogued, and systematized is to allow the construction of false systems of knowledge that do not recognize or provide a means of responding to the changing conditions of life.

The gap between demonstrable knowledge (what *is*) and contextual experience (what *seems to be*) was a central issue in ancient Greece. It became a central issue once again in eighteenth-century England, as science and philosophy laid claim to the domain of truth while leaving moral questions largely unresolved. The Sophists of ancient Greece were more concerned with 'appropriate speech or action at the appropriate time' than with any absolute, verifiable Truth. Gorgias claimed that Nature did not exist outside of human perception (or even if it did, we could not *know* it; and even if we could *know* it we could not *speak* it),[5] and Protagoras claimed that "Man is the measure of all things."[6] These thinkers were later criticized for relativism, but perhaps they were considering something very important—something that we have lost in the backwash of Plato's domination of the modern academy. Their views were grounded in the conviction that all human knowledge is, by necessity, mediated by representational processes and products: perception, thought, art, and language. They acknowledged that human beings are confined in knowing to the domain of *doxa*, or emerging opinion, that we must always respond to particular contexts (*kairos*) in ways appropriate for those contexts, and that meaning is always constructed in language and symbols (*logos*). But accepting these things does not necessarily lead to relativism and nothingness. On the contrary, such an acceptance may lead to a much more pragmatic, beautiful, and morally engaged view of the way in which we know.

To trust in kairos, rather than depending on rational analysis of every decision, is a frightening choice. It is to understand that not everything is within our rational control; to accept that the best way to learn something new may be to *do* it, even at the expense of failing over and over; and to draw on intuition as well as rational analysis as we formulate and share our experiences with others.

For Plato, such a view of experience and knowledge was entirely unacceptable. In the *Gorgias*, for example, Socrates [Plato] belittles rhetoric by claiming that it is not really an art—it is more like "cookery." Socrates says, at [463], "rhetoric seems not to be an artistic pursuit at all ... It seems to have many branches and one of them is cookery, which is thought to be an art, but according to my notion is no art at all, but a knack and a routine" (23–4). He extends this notion further on the following pages, saying that "as cookery [is] to medicine, rhetoric is to justice" and asserting that rhetoric is "the counterpart of cookery in the soul" (26). The "cookery" figure employed by Socrates implies that rhetoric is a less valuable pursuit than dialectic—a "knack" or a "routine" rather than a true "art." Like cookery, rhetoric often involves trial and error proceedings. It can be reduced to mindless, fixed recipes. It can depend on a "knack" or on intuitively developed habits. It simply cannot be considered rationally constructed, exact, and certain knowledge. And for Plato, that made it a less valuable pursuit.

What Plato did not acknowledge, of course, is that the human mind must use such "cookery" *by necessity* when confronted with the task of making choices in a complex world. Not all decisions can be reasoned through; not every action can be carefully planned. His pristine view of ideal forms and philosophical systems has always been appealing, but it has always been false in important ways.

Plato attempts to silence the Sophists in his dialogues, to assert the absolute importance of seeking and finding Truth over the importance of context-bound, day-in-day-out decision-making. But in Plato's time, and since that time, the other current of thought—coming down from the Sophists—has continued to assert the significance of a kairos-centered moral view, to value learning by practice within contexts rather than by contemplating, and to foster and value intuitive decision-making. That rhetorical current of thought has been represented by ancient thinkers such as Isocrates, Quintilian, and Longinus and modern thinkers such as Kenneth Burke and Gregory Bateson.

Wordsworth should be considered within this tradition, because from the very beginning of his career he entered the fray on the side of rhetoric. In the "Essay on Morals," he sets the tone for his later theory and practice by asserting that habits of mind are as important as reasoned decision-making, that direct experience is much more convincing than any systematic argument can ever be, and that language should be used to enter and convey experience rather than to capture and control it by assigning it to comfortable categories.

My Critical Stance and Assumptions

This text reads Wordsworth's compositions within the context of the knowledge battle discussed above, and asserts that they offer a coherent and powerful synthetic vision of the engagement of mind and world meant to complement, not displace or extend, Newtonian science. Like everyone else, I begin with some assumptions. But I am convinced that they are fair and reasonable assumptions. I assume that

1. Wordsworth's theory is about just what he says it is—Man, Nature, and Society—and not about poetry as an artifact or about his own life as an imaginative record. Wordsworth's theory, I contend, is primarily about metaphysics and epistemology—about issues that have traditionally been studied under the rubric of philosophy. And only when his theory is read with this larger order in mind can it be seen as consistent and coherent (not complete or totalizable);
2. While "rhetoric" is a term that has been much-abused by philosophers and scientists since the late seventeenth century, it can, and must, be reconstructed by returning to its rich and complex origins in the ideas of ancient Greece and Rome and by its articulation and use in theories of discourse such as the one developed in the twentieth century by Kenneth Burke;
3. Wordsworth, like all educated people of the time, participated in a rhetoric-based education, and his thinking was shaped and influenced by the ideas articulated in classical rhetoric—particularly Quintilian.[7] Because many of his contemporaries were condemning the use of rhetoric in intellectual discourse, he would have been cautious not to use the word "rhetoric" when talking about his poetic purposes and practices. But those purposes and practices are in essence rhetorical; and
4. Rhetoric, philosophy, and poetic are interrelated modes of discourse. No simple dividing lines can be drawn between them, and their relationship is complicated and recursive. For example, rhetorical modes are used to construct and gain assent for philosophical systems; poetic modes are used to exemplify and clarify philosophical concepts and to move readers by engaging them; and philosophical modes are used rhetorically to give the impression of rigor and credibility.

These assumptions make sense, but they raise complicated questions for analysis. Is it possible to judge a poem, for example, or a body of poetry, as an experiment in philosophy? I think it certainly is, but the critical tools that we can bring to bear on the task are fewer and less comfortable to use. And therefore critics have avoided the task when possible. 'As a literary critic, what do I know about philosophy?' one might ask. Or 'As a philosopher, what do I know about the forms and styles and lingo of poetry analysis?' The answer in both cases is 'Potentially a great deal, but never everything.' Which is exactly the answer that an expert in either field must give, eventually, when questioned hard enough about his or her own disciplinary knowledge.

Such questions can be very intimidating. How is it possible to know when one knows enough to venture across disciplinary boundaries? How can one know everything? These questions are framed in terms that do not allow trial and error and ongoing learning. As a result, they stop meaningful inquiry in its tracks. Why not ask questions like 'How can my field of study contribute to another field of study? How are these fields of study alike and unlike? Why don't I follow this line of thinking and see where it will lead, even if it leads me across disciplinary boundaries?' To open new avenues of significant inquiry, we must drop the pretension of being the "philosopher-kings" of a discipline and take the approach of learners attempting to make new connections.

That is the approach that I take in this text. I read Wordsworth's early poetry and prose as one unified body of writing with rhetorical, poetic, and philosophical dimensions. My analysis is not linear, but recursive. I identify patterns and then return to the development of those patterns over time and explore their broader ramifications. I explore the working of ideas in multiple contexts.

My aim is to show that Wordsworth's early writings are informed by dissatisfaction with the Enlightenment model of knowing. Indeed, contrary to much recent critical opinion, Wordsworth was very much engaged with the social ramifications of the French Revolution—but on a level that it is easy to overlook. In one surge of history, the French Revolution both epitomized the Reason-centered epistemology of the Enlightenment and revealed its absolute failure. The intellectual thread that connects Burke and Wordsworth is their intuitive understanding of this critical truth. The ideals that were betrayed by the French Revolution were broader than many critics have recognized. The lesson that we have never learned from the French Revolution, despite Burke's and Wordsworth's efforts to teach us, is that Reason is not enough. Wordsworth's *Prelude* struggles with implications of the French Revolution that have been largely overlooked. It portrays his revelation that reason itself is the problem. The terror in France did not emerge from an abandonment of reason; it was the natural result of a ruthless application of Reason.

When Wordsworth explores the mind and the way it works, and attempts to make lasting connections between the mind and the natural world, he does so at least partly in response to his sense that the epistemology that led both to the French Revolution and the Industrial Revolution in England is literally a killing epistemology. In the late 1790s, he sought a harmony and a balance that the Reasoning mind had failed to attain, and so he began his most creative phase with a profound distrust of Reason. We have interpreted this distrust in a number of ways, but as interpreters firmly entrenched in a Reason-centered epistemology, we have a very difficult time seeing it for what it is: an intelligent and questing response to the conditions of his times. In the second and third sections of this text, I examine Wordsworth's reaction to the Cartesian/Newtonian model of knowing and explore the alternative model of knowing that he developed. For the moment, I will simply sketch out my argument about Wordsworth's epistemic experiments in a few paragraphs.

Wordsworth found Godwin's view of a reason-centered approach to social and moral issues appealing in his early career, but his experiences in France made him more and more distrustful of reason as an instrument of social change. In the mid-1790s, Wordsworth began to develop an entirely different approach to the big questions of perception, knowledge, and the working of the mind: an approach that centered on epistemic rhetoric—on knowing as the making and sharing of symbolic representations—rather than on systematic rational inquiry. What was interesting about his response to physical science and the empirical approach to knowledge was, quite simply, that he accepted it wholeheartedly without accepting the reductive view of the world that it seemed to require. He did not attempt to deny the empirical basis of knowledge by asserting that a disembodied "Mind" or "Spirit" was the seat of moral judgment and action. He did not attempt to beg the question of individual perception, and all the complexities that that question stirred up. Instead, he accepted individual perception as the ground of all knowledge and then tried to find ways to connect individuals in their modes of perceiving and knowing. His approach placed mind within the web of physical processes that he called "Nature," relied on shared experience as the ground of shared knowing, and stressed the importance for his culture of maintaining and continually recreating accurate and powerful representations of experience.

In general, then, his alternative model was based on a number of intuitive understandings:

1. Reason is a secondary faculty of mind. Perception and imagination generate the representations on which reason operates.
2. The individual mind exists in a complex relationship with the larger physical processes of "Nature" and the larger rhetorical processes of "Society."
3. The process of knowing is *not* simply a process of rationally abstracting concepts from experience; it *is* a process of entering into a recursive relationship with the physical and rhetorical processes mentioned earlier.
4. Knowing cannot be understood in terms of "correctness" and "error." Instead it should be understood in terms of "composing" and "tuning."

In this formulation, "tuning" means the process of bringing nonrational participation and rational consideration into harmonious relationship. Pirsig articulates this process nicely when he describes a craftsman at work:

> The craftsman isn't ever following a single line of instruction. He's making decisions as he goes along. For that reason he'll be absorbed and attentive to what he's doing even though he doesn't deliberately contrive this. His motions and the machine are in a kind of harmony. He isn't following any set of written instructions because the nature of the material at hand determines his thoughts and motions, which simultaneously change the nature of the material at hand. The material and his thoughts are changing together in a progression of changes until his mind's at rest at the same time the material's right. (148)

Such "tuning" occurs in relationship and is akin to creative process. Its importance is acknowledged in art; Wordsworth's aim is to acknowledge it as vital to human knowing in all its contexts.

Quintilian's *Institutes of Oratory* provided Wordsworth with a conceptual model for this process of "tuning." The text centered on "composing," broadly defined to include not only invention and discovery but disposition, presentation, and even revision. It implied a model of knowing that included the processes as well as the products, the knowers as well as the known. Wordsworth's rhetorical model is founded on the belief that poesis is a critical component of knowing, that "making" or "composing" is the fundamental human activity. Like Isocrates, he asserted that human beings are, first and foremost, meaning-making animals, and that human meaning-making was always centered on the ability to use language. Poetic and rhetoric aim to reshape logos rather than to report "reality." In a model of knowing that claims "reality" is the main issue, and can be "reported," poetic and rhetoric become secondary modes of discourse. But in a model of knowing that asserts "logos" as the center, and acknowledges the limits of logos, kairos, and doxa, they remain primary modes of discourse.

By developing a logos-centered model of knowing, Wordsworth attempted to reshape and revalue poetry, to broaden his society's narrowing view of knowledge, and to reconstitute moral vision and belief in a society on its way to terminal doubt. In short, he sought to make poetry an accessible, experience-based discourse of learning and knowing.

Chapter 2
Enduring Knowledge Traditions

The whole university he was attending smelled of the same ugliness. It was everywhere, in the classroom, in the textbooks. It was in himself and he didn't know how or why. It was reason itself that was ugly and there seemed no way to get free.
—Robert Pirsig, *Zen and the Art of Motorcycle Maintenance*

Plato's work ... marks the canonization of the subject/object distinction in the West. Increasingly, the Greek began to see himself as an autonomous personality apart from his acts; as a separate consciousness rather than a series of moods.
—Morris Berman, *The Reenchantment of the World*

Positivism works out well for scientists and mathematicians, since it allows only them to speak. Everyone else utters "meaningless" statements about the world and life and morals and beauty. Problems of God and metaphysics and goodness and value reduce to mere "pseudo-problems," questions asked by those whom language has misled, those who do not know what counts as answers.
—Bart Kosko, *Fuzzy Thinking*

Introduction

Much misunderstanding of Wordsworth's "theory" and "practice" has arisen from a deeply ingrained, culturally constructed view of what constitutes knowledge. Every culture rests on a set of fundamental definitions, one of which is the definition of knowledge. In times of social upheaval or cultural paradigm change, individuals contend to reshape the central definitions of their culture. This process is, at root, both personal (driven by "subjective" views of what the world is and ought to be) and political (aimed at controlling or directing the future course of knowledge-making discourse). In order to step outside of a particular construction of knowledge, to examine it critically, one must first accept that it *is* a construction and then one must re-examine the personal and political choices that were made—the cultural forces that came to bear—as the current model of knowledge was constructed. This chapter examines the origins and the tenets of the model of knowledge that Wordsworth grappled with, examines the ways in which Wordsworth's critics, by operating within that model of knowledge, have misread and misrepresented his compositions, and finally suggests that we read Wordsworth within the context of a significant but little-discussed counter-tradition.

Knowledge is Power

'Knowledge is Power.' Since Bacon, this cliché has been a central assumption of western culture. Our stress on universal education, our insistence on the value of information, and our disdain for ignorance all come from this driving assumption. We might say in fact that colonialism itself has been driven by the conviction that 'knowledge is power' and that we, as westerners, have more of it and have a right to exercise it over others for their own good.

'Knowledge is Power.' Such a simple, straightforward statement. But it demands close examination because it connects the worlds of mind and matter, joining "Philosophy" with "Politics," "Knowing" with "Doing," "Thinking" with "Acting." And the nature of the connections it makes depends on the definition of the word "knowledge." As a culture, we tend to interpret it in linear, purely materialistic terms: "if you know how to do something, you have the power to do it." This interpretation is completely natural given our "engineering" bias—our infatuation with "know-how." It lends itself nicely to "problem-solving" approaches: if you *know* the answer, you can *solve* the problem. *Power* is seen as physical might, as technological force, as *action*.

But the statement also suggests a higher-level conceptual interpretation that is quite interesting. Might it not be said that 'Knowledge is Power' in the broadest sense that those who define what knowledge IS have near-absolute power over the forms and content of all subsequent discourse? Once the terms have been set—knowledge *is* these things, knowledge *is not* these things, knowledge *can be* reached by these steps, knowledge *cannot be reached* by these steps—the shape of all discourse that aspires to knowledge is largely set. And since only discourse that aspires to knowledge is given serious intellectual consideration in a literate culture, decisions about what knowledge *is* are highly exclusive.[1]

In our culture, for example, "literary" discourse is generally treated as "art" or "play" or "fantasy," rather than as knowledge-making discourse.

This assertion makes good sense, but it is rarely considered. For the most part, who doubts science's authority when it comes to the discovery (making) of knowledge? Strangely enough, the group of people who have the most serious doubts on this issue are scientists themselves. A handful of scientists and scientifically-trained thinkers have mustered the force to question science at the most fundamental level—its construction of what knowledge really IS—and to find that there are no easy answers to their questions. Neils Bohr's "Copenhagen Interpretation" of quantum theory basically admits that we have no way of knowing the essential nature of matter and energy, or even of knowing the "world-as-it-is." All we have is a set of tools that predict well.[2] Heisenberg's "Uncertainty Principle" acknowledges that there is a degree of uncertainty in any observation of nature. If we measure the velocity of an electron exactly, we can have no idea of its position, and vice versa. Einstein's studies of photosynthesis indicated that light has both wave- and particle-like qualities, depending on the experimental context. In short, the advances of quantum physics have shown us that the "observer" is really a participant—because the act of observing changes the system being observed—and that the way questions are framed has a major shaping effect on the experimental results. But the implications of this recent awareness have not been disseminated throughout our culture.

Once we accept the fact that knowledge is culturally defined rather than "natural," we can say some important things about epistemologies or epistemes (knowledge-making paradigms or models) in simple, pragmatic terms. First, decisions about the nature of knowledge are never "pure" of affective elements. The men and women who attempt to influence the shape of knowledge are driven by their own needs and desires and hopes as much as they are driven by their quest for "Truth." Jasper Neel illuminates this very nicely in *Plato, Derrida, and Writing*. Plato's intellectual program was not simply a "search for Truth." It was founded on significant politicosocial value assumptions, and it was presented forcefully in an effort to enlist others, by direct or indirect persuasion, in its assault on previously accepted forms of knowledge (more on this in a few pages).

Second, there can be no epistemology without metaphysics. In order to discuss the processes and products of human knowing, we must make some assumptions about the "world-as-it-is." We must start with beliefs—about cosmology, about human nature, about our place in the universe—in order to begin developing an understanding of human knowledge and its value in the scheme of things.

Third, knowledge-making is always a political process. The epistemology of a culture influences (and limits) individual choices, institutions, and legislative decisions.

To examine models of knowledge effectively, we must keep these terms of knowledge-making in mind and build them into our accounting. They frame the following discussion of the dilemmas that Wordsworth faced in the nineteenth and twentieth centuries.

Wordsworth the Poet, Coleridge the Philosopher-Critic: Our Cultural Predispositions at Work

Despite Arnold's warning that Wordsworth's philosophy should not be taken seriously, critics have gone to great lengths to establish clear summations of Wordsworth's philosophical position(s).[3] Why is this so? Perhaps because his compositions show so clearly that he is struggling with the large questions of how the human mind works in the world and how the world works on the mind. As readers, we simply cannot avoid this important element of his writing. But because of his apparent inconsistencies and his refusal to offer systematic expositions of his thinking, our tendency has been to consider his ideas as half-baked derivations from other sources, mostly attributable to the energizing contact he had with Coleridge.[4] The assumption has been simple: Wordsworth was the 'poet' and Coleridge the 'philosopher.' Coleridge helped to propagate this assumption by criticizing Wordsworth's failure to live up to his own theories publicly, and by suggesting that many of Wordsworth's central ideas were dependent on Coleridge's thinking.[5]

Owen and Smyser's "Introduction" to the texts of the Prefaces, for example, uses Coleridge's own authority (an interesting conflict here) to establish that Wordsworth owes a debt to Coleridge in the composition of the Prefaces. Coleridge writes:

> 'the Preface is half a Child of my own Brain & so arose out of Conversations, so

frequent, that with few exceptions we could scarcely either of us perhaps positively say, which first started any particular Thought.' (*PW* 1: 112–13)

We have little real evidence beyond this claim to suggest that the Preface was based as much on Coleridge's ideas as Wordsworth's. Perhaps Coleridge is appropriating Wordsworth's original ideas as much as Wordsworth supposedly appropriates his? The nature of the collaboration between the two authors remains open to debate. Their conversations certainly provoked Wordsworth to a fuller consideration in prose of his principles and purposes in writing poetry; but it could very well be that Coleridge provided a point of opposition which Wordsworth used to define his own positions. The different patterns of development in the work of the two men, and their early divergence on important poetic principles, makes it much more likely that the two were engaged by similar purposes, but with differing assumptions and ideas about how to attain the ends they sought. It is safe to say that Coleridge was not the "source" of the final complex of ideas that Wordsworth assembled—though he performed the valuable service of helping Wordsworth to articulate that complex.

In general, Wordsworth's work shows very different patterns of thinking than Coleridge's. It took years for those differences to grow into tensions that divided the two men, but Wordsworth recognized them very early. In fact, he began to show his desire to be free of Coleridge's considerable shadow as early as the 1800 Preface to *Lyrical Ballads*. In the 1798 Advertisement he acknowledged Coleridge as a co-creator of the collection, and expressed a sense of indebtedness to him, writing that

> For the sake of variety and from a consciousness of my own weakness I was induced to request the assistance of a Friend, who furnished me with the Poems of the ANCIENT MARINER, the FOSTER-MOTHER'S TALE, the NIGHTINGALE, the DUNGEON, and the Poem entitled LOVE. I should not, however, have requested this assistance, had I not believed that the poems of my Friend would in a great measure have the same tendency as my own, and that, though there would be found a difference, there would be found no discordance in the colours of our style; as our opinions on the subject of Poetry do almost entirely coincide. (*PW* 1: 119–20)

In the 1800 Preface, however, he replaced this passage with one that changes the tone toward Coleridge considerably:

> It is proper to inform the Reader that the Poems entitled the ancient Mariner, the Foster Mother's Tale, the Nightingale, the Dungeon, and Love, are written by a friend, who has also furnished me with a few of those Poems in the second volume, which are classed under the title of "Poems on the Naming of Places." (*PW* 1: 120n).

The change is indicative. Wordsworth does not allude to his need for "assistance" in the revised version, and he makes no attempt to connect Coleridge's ideas concerning Poetry with his own any longer. This alteration, I think, is at least a first step by Wordsworth toward independence from Coleridge and his ideas.

Yet as Bialostosky has shown, we still misread Wordsworth by examining his compositions through a filter of Coleridge's ideas.[6] And we tend to measure Wordsworth's successes as a poet in terms of Coleridge's systematic critique in the *Biographia Literaria*. Coleridge writes in a philosophical, expository style that we can understand. Wordsworth's prose is tangled and dense and obtuse. As a result, Coleridge has too often set a poor course for Wordsworth criticism.

I discuss the Wordsworth/Coleridge relationship, and the way it has shaped our understanding of Wordsworth's work, to illustrate a larger set of cultural predispositions about knowledge and poetry and discourse that have been deeply-entrenched for centuries. Our culture separates philosophical or scientific knowledge—knowledge of what *is*—from poetry and rhetoric, which deal with appearances and imaginative worlds. In order to qualify as knowledge, ideas must be organized into linear and hierarchical systems of thinking which must be internally consistent and which must have significant predictive power. While this sounds fine on the surface, in practice it leads to a more and more narrow definition of what can be "known." Everything is divided into "demonstrable knowledge" on the one hand and "personal perception" on the other. And that means that art and poetry and music and law and a thousand other human pursuits may not qualify as real knowledge. By choosing poetry as his primary mode of expression, Wordsworth has made it very hard for his readers to accept the fact that he has something significant to say about human knowing.

To illustrate this point, I return briefly to Owen and Smyser's "Introduction" to the texts of the Preface to *Lyrical Ballads*. They write that the Preface

> is Wordsworth's best known critical work, and his most original essay in aesthetics, in the sense that it often appears to be the result of his introspective examination of his own poetic processes. It is less original than has sometimes been thought, however, in that many of its aesthetic, psychological, and sociological presuppositions are quite commonplace, especially in the numerous writings on aesthetics in English which appeared during the eighteenth century, based often on the associationist psychology of Locke and Hartley or on the primitivistic theories of culture and literature which are characteristic of the Scottish "Common-sense" philosophers. It is only rarely possible to point to specific sources, but our Commentary makes clear Wordsworth's general debt to the eighteenth century. (*PW* 1: 112).

I quote at length to represent fully the way Wordsworth's ideas are typically screened as a result of our cultural view of knowledge. Owen and Smyser assert that they are "quite commonplace," based on a number of existing "presuppositions," and that they are limited to "aesthetics." Built into this passage is the assumed division between "theories of culture and literature," on the one hand, and philosophy or science on the other. A theory of culture or literature can be "based on" psychology, but cannot *be* psychology.

To understand why such a view of Wordsworth is inappropriate, we must reconsider some definitions and assumptions. First, any assertion that a set of ideas is based on a number of "existing presuppositions" is tautological. Of course a set of ideas is based on, or at least holds dialogue with, intellectual presuppositions that have already been worked out. The question of the value of ideas has little to do with this fact. That question—"are these ideas valuable and significant?"—has more to do with the quality of the selection, the dialogue, and the synthesis that is carried out beginning with those presuppositions. Wordsworth certainly drew on many sources in the eighteenth century for terminology and a conceptual foothold, but he employed those sources in ways that were largely unheard of. He intermixed selected ideas of the eighteenth century with a firm grounding in classical rhetoric, and created a model of mindfulness and poetic purpose all his own. His originality was a matter of synthesis more than analysis.

And second, we must understand that Wordsworth would not accept the limited view of "aesthetics" that our cultural predispositions encourage us to take. Aesthetics is a field of study that has traditionally dealt with the principles of defining, recognizing, and appreciating beauty. We tend to limit the study of aesthetics to issues of "style," which all too often has been defined in opposition to "substance," and to issues of "taste," which all too often has been defined in trivial and elitist terms. Wordsworth tries, again and again, to make it abundantly clear in his Prefaces that he is talking about something much larger than "aesthetics," in this very limited sense. He insists that "taste," for example, is not an arbitrary and fickle requirement for membership in an elite group, but is a fundamental category of good judgment. In the 1802 Preface, for example, he mocks those

> who talk of Poetry as of a matter of amusement and idle pleasure; who will converse with us as gravely about a taste for Poetry, as they express it, as if it were a thing as indifferent as a taste for rope-dancing, or Frontiniac or Sherry. (*PW* 1: 139)

And his dismissal of eighteenth-century poetic diction and language choices is based on the same broad view of aesthetics. He makes this distinction carefully in the 1800 Preface, stating that he aims to use a language of "real men" because

> such a language arising out of repeated experience and regular feelings is a more permanent and a far more philosophical language than that which is frequently substituted for it by Poets, who think that they are conferring honour upon themselves and their art in proportion as they separate themselves from the sympathies of men, and indulge in arbitrary and capricious habits of expression in order to furnish food for fickle tastes and fickle appetites of their own creation. (*PW* 1: 124)

Beauty emerges from and informs experience—it cannot be a separate category for discussion. To insist that the Preface is only about aesthetics is like insisting that Einstein's theory of relativity is only about aesthetics. Both documents are concerned with wholeness and harmony of vision, and so both are certainly concerned with aesthetics. But neither limits itself to that issue. Both are also about life and how we conduct it well (and represent it well) within a puzzling universe. Einstein is read with great seriousness because he speaks the language of Science, while Wordsworth is generally dismissed as a serious thinker because he speaks the language of Poetry.

Wordsworth has been a victim of a cultural predisposition to see systematic thinking, even if it is poorly done, as a valid source of knowledge, and to see poetry as an entertainment. To re-examine Wordsworth's compositions, we must first re-examine a deeply ingrained, culturally constructed view of what constitutes knowledge. And that means we must return, at least briefly, to a knowledge battle waged in the fifth century B.C.E.

Plato's Bid for Knowledge-Power

The academy seems to have forgotten that a serious battle was waged in ancient Greece in the fifth century B.C.E. over the issue of human knowing and the limits of that knowing. We have canonized the work of Plato, accepting rather uncritically that his writings represent the emergence of rational inquiry and the 'philosophic mind.' In *Plato, Derrida, and Writing*, Jasper Neel complicates that canonization by suggesting that Plato had other motives than the "pursuit of Truth." Neel claims that Plato's texts represent an attempt to appropriate writing, and discourse in general, for Plato's own "philosophical" ends. Our reverence for Plato shows that he was largely successful; however, our postmodern "knowledge establishment" and the conditions of life that have emerged from it suggest that his success has not proven beneficial to us.

In theory, the Platonic model suggests that knowledge comes from sustained and critical inquiry, from the questioning and answering and requestioning that Plato called "dialectic." In Plato's textual practice, however, knowledge is something first to be possessed and then exercised. Plato's predisposition is to value research and study first, and to value human activity only as it is guided by such research and study. This Platonic predisposition has shaped the modern academy, which despite giving lip service to the importance of teaching really stresses research and "discovery" as the defining features of scholarship (and knowing). "Getting" knowledge is the primary task, and then all that remains is teaching it to others and/or applying it in particular contexts. Of course, we only "get" knowledge through contextually-bound activity—whether that activity is teaching, community involvement, or research. But that phase of the process is often ignored. All too often, the genuine dialectic of learning, in which teacher and student dance together in an ongoing process, becomes magisterial dialectic, a game played by those who already know with those who do not know but may have a chance of "getting there."

Was Socrates ever proven wrong? Did he ever learn anything? Where did his knowledge come from in the first place? Did he ever *do* anything—travel, raise a family, engage in public affairs, and so on— besides enlighten the minds of the young men who played the dialectic game with him? None of these questions bear close examination if one wishes to take the Platonic model of dialectic seriously. For Socrates' record makes him look very much like a "Sophist" in the negative sense of the word that he himself employs.[7] He spends all his time engaged in contention, showing off his knowledge to underlings and using (highly rhetorical) language to force others to accept his views. He does not accept money for his services, or so it seems, but that 'purity' does not save him from the faults of Sophism. His appeal lies completely in his rational and linguistic mastery, not in the pragmatic or moral value of his knowledge or his methods. And Plato is the stage manager who makes that mastery inevitable. We never see Socrates struggling with loss or grief or making difficult decisions; we never see him caring for children or creating something other than an argument. We never see him make a mistake. He has been canonized as a *master*, as one who *knows*. And that denies everything that the theory of dialectic sets forth.

Dialectic is supposed to be an interaction between two or more people desiring to know, guided by careful and thoughtful questioning, moving in the direction of Truth. It becomes in Plato's texts, however, a completely magisterial situation in which Socrates manipulates the views of straw men who cannot construct arguments as well as he can. Once one party is a master, dialectic ends. Therefore, there is little or no dialectic in the dialogues of Plato. Socrates is the product, but the *process* is not revealed. We are often left with the impression that he is a master toying with the untutored. His aim, it seems, is not to participate in an ongoing learning process but to "transmit" knowledge to the misguided.

This paradigm should sound familiar to those who are aware of contemporary composition theory and research. It is an exact match of what Maxine Hairston popularized as the "current-traditional" academic model. A teacher "knows" and "gives" that knowledge to students, who must accept the mastery of the teacher and the knowledge they are "given." There is little understanding of pedagogy, and the practice of teaching is considered to be secondary, less important, than the "research" and "theory" that lead to "new knowledge." There are those who *know* (teachers) and those who *do not know* (students).

Something important is missing here. How does one decide what is *worth* knowing? How does one engage others in the *process* of knowing? How does one *apply* the knowledge gained in significant real-life situations? The Platonic model does not address these questions, and the modern academy is only now discovering and exploring them with concern and purpose.

The Platonic model is highly attractive to introspective intellectuals, but it contains a creeping ugliness that must be recognized and synthesized in order for us to use Platonic texts well. It simply dismisses responsibility and labor and suffering—the elements required for personal and public learning and growth—from the field of human inquiry. It offers intellectual power and mastery, but only with the condition of, and at the cost of, personal withdrawal from the complexities of physical and affective existence. In the *Symposium*, for example, Plato's position is represented by Aristophanes, who applauds homosexuality because it enables men to avoid the complications of heterosexual involvement and parenting. In the *Republic*, Plato effectively eliminates artists and poets from the state. The Platonic model frees and enshrines Reason, but denies the possibility of affective knowledge and imaginative vision. Plato wants to have the final word, as Neel suggests.

An alternative model of knowledge was available in Plato's time, however: a model that illuminates Plato's position considerably and that may provide us with better grounds for knowing. This model faced directly the limitations of human knowledge and the importance of constructing knowledge in the world of loving, suffering, and longing beings. I hope to complicate our canonization of Plato's work a bit further by submitting the contemplative model of knowledge that it puts forth to the social and moral criticism implied in the work of a little-known contemporary thinker: Isocrates.

A Forgotten Voice

Despite its rootedness in Classical thinking, the Enlightenment model of knowledge largely ignored a persistent but quiet voice coming down from ancient Athens. Isocrates has vanished from intellectual consideration for many hundreds of years, yet his wisdom remains as an undercurrent in the world of ideas even today. He was a teacher, a contemporary of Plato, who had a very different viewpoint on language and knowledge from the one held by his competitor. Plato's vitriol against "rhetoric," expressed in the *Gorgias* and the *Phaedrus*, was at least in part vitriol against this highly successful Athenian teacher who was proposing methods and ideas that Plato found offensive and threatening. Isocrates' ideas dominated education for over sixteen hundred years until the "rediscovery" of Plato and Aristotle changed the face of knowledge.[8] Indeed, the Isocratean position has existed and been argued for ever since the two men did "battle" for supremacy in ancient Athens.

In general terms, Isocrates offered a model that stressed *praxis* rather than *theoria*. While Plato constructed a model in which one would know first and then act with full authority, Isocrates insisted that "knowing" emerged primarily from action itself. The difference is simple, yet absolutely vital.

The Platonic position places less value on practical experience, for it stresses the mastery of principles, of truths, by way of critical inquiry. The Platonic ideal valorizes contemplation—years gathering and examining knowledge—and implies that action and public engagement are secondary issues in terms of both time and value. For Plato, "episteme" and "phronesis" were related as teacher and student. One would strive to master truths before applying them in practice.

The Isocratean position, on the other hand, places practical experience in a place of the utmost importance. Indeed, Isocrates claimed in "Against the Sophists" that formal training, and Platonic "contemplation," were the secondary issues:

> For ability, whether in speech or in any other activity, is found in those who are well endowed by nature and have been schooled by practical experience. Formal training makes such men more skilful [sic] and more resourceful ... But it cannot fully fashion men who are without natural aptitude into good debaters or writers... (2: 173).

In general, his pedagogy placed *doing* first and facilitated the evolution of understanding within the context of doing. For him "episteme" (or demonstrable knowledge) was of less concern than "phronesis" (or practical wisdom). In the *Antidosis*, he says bluntly

> I hold that men who want to do some good in the world must banish utterly from their interests all vain speculations and all activities which have no bearing on our lives. (2: 335)

And he refines the concept a bit further on, saying

> I hold that what some people call philosophy is not entitled to that name ... For since it is not in the nature of man to attain a science by the possession of which we can know positively what we should do or what we should say, in the next resort I hold that man to be wise who is able by his powers of conjecture to arrive generally at the best course, and I hold that man to be a philosopher who occupies himself with the studies from which he will most quickly gain that kind of insight. (2: 335)

Isocrates is subject to criticism of at least two sorts here: he does not directly address the issue of "vision" or "imagination," so how can things ever improve if we simply accept what is "real" and work practically within that arena? And he makes it possible to distort his central reasoning into "sophism": as Sebberson says, a "smooth calculus between ends and means" which has no firm moral conviction.[9]

But these two problems can be resolved by an appeal to logos—or to "symbolic reality." If "reality" is a process rather than a "final state," then knowing can have no endpoint. The philosopher, according to Isocrates, is not the person with the greatest collection of abstract knowledge, but the person who has best developed and refined his or her *readiness* for the next situation-at-hand, for the ever-changing kairos.

And the only "firm moral conviction" that matters is moral conviction that operates within the specific contexts of life. For example, the commandment "Thou shalt not kill" represents a powerful and significant moral position. But if one is confronted with a situation in which one has the choice of killing someone or watching that person kill another person, or a large number of persons, one may choose morally to take life in order to preserve life. A firm awareness of context is always required in order to make moral decisions.

This difficult and important distinction is raised by Carol Gilligan in our own time, when she sketches out a morality of *responsibility* to counter what Piaget has described as a morality of *rights*. The predominant (male) view of our culture has been that moral issues should be decided "blindly" and "objectively" on the basis of principles and moral reasoning (Gilligan, in Belenky et al 8). But if morality begins with relationship, in context, and with careful representation of the situation-at-hand, then logos provides the resolution. Only by speaking and thinking well in contexts can we attain a moral stance. Indeed, as Isocrates (and later Quintilian and Wordsworth) recognized, speaking and thinking well in contexts *leads to* morality. Good habits of perception and speaking, of knowing, lead to moral action.

At the center of the Isocratean approach is an awareness that human knowledge is contextual and limited to the domain of experience, and that the only knowledge that has real value is knowledge that emerges from and has use within the moral quagmire of daily life. These ideas makes good sense, but they do not "fit" the way that our culture has constructed knowledge from medieval times to our own.

Our culture has followed the Platonic lead, choosing the path toward independence, stressing the distancing of self from the known, and accepting that there is a hierarchy of knowledge running from sensory experience at the "bottom" to universalized abstractions at the "top." We have, like Plato, valorized the movement towards universals and abstract formulations and condemned or demeaned the movement towards perception and sensation. And although this model of knowing has helped us consolidate vast power in the methods and products of science and technology, it has also created many severe cultural and personal problems.

Today's De(con)structive Model of Knowledge

In the last decade of the twentieth century, Western culture remains under the sway of the mode of thinking which Morris Berman calls the "Cartesian paradigm" (24), but which can be traced back to the fusing of Platonic and Aristotelian values. This mode of thinking generates (and is generated by) dualisms and dichotomies such as "inside" and "outside," "self" and "world," and "subjective" and "objective." The terms "outside," "world," and "objective" are privileged—even revered—in our culture, because they seem to represent an escape from egotism, self-interest, and self-delusion into an (idealized) realm of "reality" that exists independent of the "doubt" inherent in human perception and value judgments. The "Cartesian paradigm" is a mode of thinking that emerges from what I call "Philosophy" in this book. "Truth" is its goal; "Fact" is its standard; "Science" is its method.

It does not matter whether one takes the more empirical stance favored by Aristotle or the more rationalist stance favored by Plato, because both stances share the Philosophical removal of "real knowledge" from the world of doxa—opinion, practical experience, and so on—by way of generalization, categorization, and/or dialectic questioning. Both seek a knowledge that is free from the uncertainties of our daily existence in social and personal relations. Despite their differences, philosophical "empiricism" and "rationalism" both place knowledge "outside" or "beyond" experience itself. For the empiricist, knowledge is attained by way of experience, but it still exists prior to and independent of any "personal" or "subjective" aspects of experience. For the rationalist, knowledge is attained by enlightenment from without, by method, by intuition, by something that transcends daily experience. Both question or dismiss the value of perceptual experience by asserting that it is only a means to the end of abstract and general knowledge, rather than a valuable end in itself.

Our dominant model of intellectual inquiry and knowledge remains Philosophical—the same as it was for the early followers of Descartes, Newton, and Locke. The only way to know anything is to remove it from its context (including, of course, its relation with "self") and to study it impartially as "itself" by way of careful observation and systematic analysis. Even with the "new" (most of a century old, but still little-discussed) awareness of quantum physics that "observers" are participants who shape events by their mode of questioning, even with a gradual movement toward models of intellectual inquiry and knowledge that require participation and process-oriented thought (anthropology, ethnography, composition theory, and others), we continue to construct our view of the world using the "Cartesian paradigm" as a filter.

Berman's *The Reenchantment of the World* argues convincingly that our "Cartesian" mode of thinking has had devastating cultural results. He cites the loss of "participating consciousness"—of a sense of integration between "self" and "world"—as the central problem engendered by the "Cartesian paradigm." We continue to participate fully in many cases—when listening to music, writing, watching a movie, making love—but we are unable to accept that participation as valid knowledge in and of itself. Berman claims that the

> consciousness of official culture dictates my 'recognition' that I am not, and can never be, my experiences. Whereas my premodern counterpart felt, and saw, that he was his experiences—that his consciousness was not some special, independent consciousness—I classify my own participation as some form of 'recreation,' and see reality in terms of the inspection and evaluation Plato hoped men would achieve. I thus see myself as an island, whereas my medieval or ancient predecessor saw himself more like an embryo. (77)

The intense difficulty of this position is embodied in various forms in the literature of Western culture from the mid-nineteenth century to the present. Isolation, alienation, paralysis, fragmentation—all the buzzwords of modernism—can be traced to the loss of immediate, participating consciousness as a valid form of knowledge and identity.

Berman asserts that our culture has made some critical metaphysical and epistemological errors, and that they have led to an untenable worldview in which meaning and value cannot be established except in "subjective" terms, in which both cultural and personal identity are threatened by meaninglessness, and in which individuals have no sense of how they "fit in" and no larger principles for making moral choices.

Berman's broad view of the history of science suggests that our culture's epistemological and metaphysical problems are a natural extension of the ones that Wordsworth encountered in the 1790s. And that broad view suggests two things of the utmost importance for scholars interested in Wordsworth, in discourse theory, in pragmatic epistemology, and in pedagogy:

1. Our appraisals of Wordsworth have been made using the assumptions of the very epistemological framework that he was attempting to undermine and alter. As a result, they have "missed the point." We must now attempt to construct and work within a different epistemological framework—the one suggested by Wordsworth—in order to account more fully for what he was trying to do and to place a value on it.
2. Because Wordsworth's aims and principles have been misunderstood in important ways, we must give his model of knowing a fair hearing whether it is comfortable or not. His struggles are

relevant to our contemporary world, and given the crisis that Berman and many other writers cite, it seems wise—even urgently needed—to examine the problems of knowing and constructing meaning that Wordsworth faced, and to explore the alternative paths of knowing that he offered.

Wordsworth began writing at a time of epistemic crisis: a time when intellectual and moral inquiry were becoming entirely separate fields of knowing, with potentially devastating results. David Hume recognized this problem in his later work, after pursuing abstract formulations of human perception and knowledge far into the realm of philosophical skepticism. John Danford's book *Hume and the Problem of Reason* suggests that Hume felt the moral necessity to return to the "ground" of daily experience, to leave behind philosophical abstractions that offered no sense of how individuals should *act* in a world in which systematic philosophical knowledge was uncertain at best. Danford writes that Hume saw "the necessity for rejoining science and experience" (11), and that by doing so he eventually attained a "corrected philosophical stance" which

> overcomes debilitating philosophical skepticism by returning to 'common life' or what would today be called prephilosophical consciousness, as a kind of ballast, or 'gross earthly mixture' which forestalls the philosophic tendency to rise into the ether. (11)

That "corrected philosophical stance" was implied in his later work, but it received much less attention than his earlier writings that took philosophical skepticism to its far extremes.

When Wordsworth began writing poetry in the 1790s, he faced many of the questions that had troubled Hume so deeply: how can we understand and trust individual perception? How can we be sure of the continuity of our own identity? How can we establish foundations for value and moral judgment? And he also faced another pressing question that had been implied in the late eighteenth-century discussions of "originality" and "genius": how can "originality" or human creativity exist in a mechanical world like the one so forcefully described by Newton?

In the remainder of this text, I argue that Wordsworth's early compositions are best read as an emerging response to these questions.

Indeed, these "experimental" compositions—including the "Essay on Morals," the *Lyrical Ballads*, and the Prefaces—can only be understood fully when viewed as a discursive effort to add or reclaim a dimension of human knowing that Wordsworth feared was being lost in his day. I do not attempt to extend this claim to cover the entire body of Wordsworth's later compositions, but I suggest that it might be a useful project to do so. He did not set out to create a systematic theory to oppose science, but to find a way to broaden the views of knowing being taken and to establish some clear principles for new ways of knowing. He was faced with a huge and daunting task, because of the limits of the language he used and the strongly-held views of "real knowledge" that were typical of his times. Yet he approached the task with great seriousness and with ongoing discipline, though without the plans or program of research that would have allowed him to label his efforts "science" or "philosophy."

While he flirted with the term "philosophy" when describing his work, he was more interested in defining himself as a poet, defining poetry, and defining the poet's role in his contemporary culture. As the Cambridge episode in *The Prelude* indicates, he made a conscious choice to be an artist rather than a scholar. But he did not accept that such a choice removed him from the field of knowledge-making. Robert Frost's "The Figure a poem makes" states that both artists and scholars

> work from knowledge; but ... they differ most importantly in the way their knowledge is come by. Scholars get theirs with conscientious thoroughness along projected lines of logic; poets theirs cavalierly and as it happens in and out of books. They stick to nothing deliberately, but let what will stick to them like burrs where they walk in the fields. (395)

As an artist, Wordsworth relied on his experiences as the ground of knowledge and worked from purposes that were "more felt than seen ahead like a prophecy" (Frost 395). As Wordsworth himself said in the Prefaces, every poem had a purpose—but a purpose that was not "formally conceived" before the poem was written. The purposes of creative discourse emerge during and after the act of composition. The job of this text is to reconstruct Wordsworth's artistic 'logic' looking "backward, in retrospect, after the act" (Frost 395).

And that, of course, is the way all patterns of meaning are established. Our logos is always being composed after-the-fact, representing the unknown as the known. Once composed, the logos can become heavy and hard to move. It can, indeed, begin to seem like "reality" itself. The symbolically-constructed "reality" takes the place of the sensory "reality" that it describes, and we can then be deluded (1) with the power of our predictions (which are, of course, reflected in the logos) OR (2) with the futility of our own role in constructing the logos (because it looks so final). But the logos is always being renegotiated, remade. Every voice has the potential to alter it—does alter it. And we can all participate in its renewal if we only listen and participate fully in our experiences.

Wordsworth's Critique of Systematic Knowing

To meet the challenges before us our notions of cosmology and of the general nature of reality must have room in them to permit a consistent account of consciousness.
—David Bohm, *Wholeness and the Implicate Order*

value systems hold us (*all* of us, not merely 'intellectuals') together, and when these systems start to crumble, so do the individuals who live by them.
—Morris Berman, *The Reenchantment of the World*

life is valuable—when
completed by the imagination. And
then only.
—William Carlos Williams, *Imaginations*

Chapter 3
Exploring the Limits of Reason and Rational Systems

> ...questioning the hegemony of scientific method over practical reasoning is a topic in current philosophical debate. But it can also be seen as a topic in romantic studies.
> —David Sebberson, "Practical Reasoning"

The "Disenchantment" of Mechanical Philosophy

In the seventeenth and eighteenth centuries, concepts of both self and world had undergone rapid change under the pressure of philosophical and scientific inquiry. Newtonian science had revolutionized the understanding of "matter in motion" and initiated cultural changes that would alter the face of the earth. Locke and Hume had attempted to establish empirical approaches to the study of the human mind. The issues of perception, language, and value were very troublesome to both thinkers, and with good reason. They were forced to return to the central philosophical question that Descartes had begged centuries before: how can the perceiving, understanding human self be placed in a clear and satisfying relationship with a world made up of "matter in motion"?[1] And in their attempts to answer that question, both philosophers found themselves threatened by solipsism and the dismantling of human identity. Then, as now, the human understanding of physical forces and engineering was much greater than the human understanding of what mind is and how it works.

Morris Berman claims that

> The story of the modern epoch, at least on the level of mind, is one of progressive disenchantment. From the sixteenth century on, mind has been progressively expunged from the phenomenal world. At least in theory, the reference points for all scientific explanation are matter and motion—what historians of science refer to as the "mechanical philosophy." (16)

He asserts that our dominant mode of thinking now has evolved from the mode that originated with Descartes in the sixteenth century. That mode, he claims, "can best be described as disenchantment, nonparticipation, for it insists on a rigid distinction between observer and observed" (16–17). The result of such a mode of thinking is alienation and depression, a sense of pervasive personal meaninglessness:

> Scientific consciousness is alienated consciousness: there is no ecstatic merger with nature, but rather total separation from it. Subject and object are always seen in opposition to each other. I am not my experiences, and thus not really a part of the world around me. The logical endpoint of this world view is a feeling of total reification: everything is an object, alien, not-me; and I am ultimately an object too, an alienated "thing" in a world of other, equally meaningless things. (17)

Central to what Berman calls "scientific consciousness" are views of reason as an instrument used to manipulate reality and of nature as a physical field to be manipulated. The removal of purposiveness from creation as a whole (dismissal of teleological explanations) left purpose in the hands of "mind":

> once natural processes are stripped of immanent purpose, there is really nothing left in objects but their value for something, or someone, else. Max Weber called this attitude of mind *zweckrational*, that is, purposively rational, or instrumentally rational. Embedded within the scientific program is the concept of manipulation as the very touchstone of truth. To know something is to control it... (40)

Here Berman asserts that the maxim "knowledge is power" has taken on a new meaning in the modern world. Following the technological program of Bacon, western culture has tended to focus on questions of *how* to do things, and to avoid or ignore questions of *why* we should, or should not, do those things. Questions of truth have been separated from questions of value. As Berman and others have claimed, "the medieval Thomistic (Christian-Aristotelian) synthesis, that saw the good and the true as identical, was, in the first decades of the seventeenth century, irrevocably dismantled" (40). Facts and theories have been considered valid "objective" concerns; values have been considered "subjective" or personal. The domain of rational inquiry has been reduced, and we have gradually moved toward an engineering-centered epistemology.

For Wordsworth, this trend was disastrous. In his view, the intellectual constructs of the eighteenth century had failed to maintain vital connections between human rationality, narrowly defined, and the broader fields of human creativity, personal meaning, and moral purpose. He felt that in order to integrate "objective" knowledge and "personal" knowledge, a more comprehensive view of the human mind and its relationship to a changing world was needed. In a letter to John Scott dated 11 June 18[16], Wordsworth wrote

> All men of first rate genius have been as distinguished for dignity, beauty, and propriety of moral conduct. But we often find the faculties and qualities of the mind not well balanced; something of prime importance is left short, and hence confusion and disorder... (*LWW* 190–91)

Here Wordsworth connects intellect and "dignity, beauty, and propriety of moral conduct"—a connection that illuminates his work. His explorations of the developing self in *The Prelude* and much of his other poetry are guided by his sense that the "faculties and qualities of the mind" are "not well balanced" when the reasoning intellect is isolated from beauty, creativity, and moral action. He makes a dedicated effort to restore this "something of prime importance" that is "left short," not in the isolated human mind, but in the relationship of that mind to the world around it.

In the next section, with this broader context in mind, I examine two of the formative experiences that Wordsworth dramatizes in *The Prelude*: his stay at Cambridge and his effort to overcome the despair caused by the failure of the French revolution. I contend that Wordsworth's turning away from the existing knowledge establishment, as represented by Cambridge in *The Prelude*, should be seen not as a rejection of learning but as a rejection of a failing epistemology. And Wordsworth's account of the French Revolution and its monumental failure indicates that he is concerned primarily with the inadequacy of instrumental reason as a tool of social intervention. For Wordsworth, the developing scientific epistemology failed miserably when it attempted to apply instrumental reason to the world of social and moral affairs.

The French Revolution was a vast social experiment which emerged from the growing conviction that new social and moral orders could—and should—be built upon the foundation of human reason, without regard for traditions and customs and habits. As a failed experiment, it revealed something important about the prevailing epistemology of those (and our) times—something still largely unrecognized despite the powerful and thought-provoking analyses of Burke, Wordsworth and others. Stated simply, cultures have a "mind" of their own, and instrumental reason is not an adequate tool for understanding or changing such "minds."

The Problem of Reason

Though Wordsworth's concept of imagination has often been discussed, and his philosophy argued about at length, his concept of reason as a faculty of mind has not been investigated nearly as well. The primary discussions of Wordsworth's concept of reason have involved *The Borderers*, with the general conclusion that the play represents either an outright rejection or a severe questioning of Godwin's faith in reason. Whether or not Wordsworth had a strong desire early in his career to trust in reason as the guiding faculty of the human mind, it is clear that his work as a whole shows an ambivalence towards reason that is rooted in his moral sensibility. How can the reasoning faculty of a Rivers/Oswald, or of the revolutionaries in France, be expected to form a moral foundation for social order? And if it cannot, what can? The central question of *The Borderers*—"can the intellect yield true moral judgments?" (Hartman 765)—resonates through much of Wordsworth's poetry as well.

In the well-known crisis that occurs in Book 10/11 of *The Prelude*, Wordsworth dramatizes the epistemic choices that emerge from this question. While the drama centers on his personal struggles, these epistemic choices have significant social implications of which Wordsworth was obviously aware. During this crisis, he seeks "Right reason," the crowning faculty that helps humans to judge good and evil as well as truth and falsehood, but he finds only discursive reasoning and argumentation that have little or no power to resolve moral issues. He writes that he was

> betrayed
> By present objects, and by reasonings false
> From the beginning, inasmuch as drawn
> Out of a heart which had been turned aside
> From Nature by external accidents,
> And which was thus confounded more and more,
> Misguiding and misguided. (1805 *Prelude* 10: 882–88)[2]

Reason has betrayed him because he started out wrong and "turned aside / From Nature." The passage reflects Wordsworth's awareness that it is possible to "argue right from wrong principles," that reasoning can become totally divorced from the practical realm of experience, and that such a state is a form of madness.[3] This is the problem presented by Rivers/Oswald in *The Borderers* as well; he argues convincingly from a basis of falsehood and creates a world of his own reasonings in an attempt to sway Mortimer/Marmaduke.

Like Mortimer/Marmaduke, Wordsworth falls into skepticism, confusion, and inaction when he loses faith in reason. He is

>   endlessly perplexed
> With impulse, motive, right and wrong, the ground
> Of moral obligation—what the rule,
> And what the sanction—till, demanding proof,
> And seeking it in every thing, I lost
> All feeling of conviction, and, in fine,
> Sick, wearied out with contrarieties,
> Yielded up moral questions in despair
> (1805 *Prelude* 10: 893–900)

Wordsworth concludes that arguments and proofs are not enough to answer, or even to address validly, "moral questions." But that conclusion leaves him without an epistemic "foundation." He amplifies this concern in the 1850 *Prelude* by adding a significant passage:

> This was the crisis of that strong disease,
> This the soul's last and lowest ebb; I drooped,
> Deeming our blessed reason of least use
> Where wanted most: 'The lordly attributes
> Of will and choice', I bitterly exclaimed,
> 'What are they but a mockery of a Being
> Who hath in no concerns of his a test
> Of good and evil; knows not what to fear
> Or hope for, what to covet or to shun;
> And who, if those could be discerned, would yet
> Be little profited, would see, and ask
> Where is the obligation to enforce? (1850 *Prelude* 11: 306–17)

Again, "something of prime importance" is "left short." Not only does the reason of science and systematic argument fail to maintain a firm grasp on moral issues; it also fails to provide a strong enough motive for action. Its arguments may be admired, even agreed upon, but they do not necessarily lead to positive action.4

Wordsworth senses the imminent breakdown of Right Reason in his time. In the 1600s, Milton could still believe that

> The function of the human mind as a whole is to know; the function of the faculty of reason or judgment is to discriminate between true or false things to be done, or between right and wrong. (Hoopes 4)

But Wordsworth has no such assurance about reason's power as a faculty of moral judgment. In fact, his crisis in Book 10/11 of *The Prelude* arises from a frustrated longing for Right Reason, for a faculty that "presides with equal validity and certainty over the realms of intellect and morality" (Hoopes 4). In 1805, he writes

>   great God,
> Who send'st thyself into this breathing world
> Through Nature and through every kind of life,
> And mak'st man what he is, creature divine,
> In single or in social eminence,
> Above all these raised infinite ascents
> When reason, which enables him to be,
> Is not sequestered— (1805 *Prelude* 10: 385–92)

Clearly Wordsworth, like his predecessors, considers intellect and rationality to be the gifts of God that set man apart from the beasts. But he does not trust in reason "sequestered" from the world of human experience, from moral judgment, or from meaningful action. He simply cannot trust in the reasoning faculty that allowed (or even led to) the horrors of the French Revolution.

The failure of the ideals of the French Revolution is directly connected to images of reason in the final lines of this passage,

>   when the sun,
> That rose in splendour, was alive, and moved
> In exaltation among living clouds,
> Hath put his function and his glory off,
> And, turned into a gewgaw, a machine,
> Sets like an opera phantom. (1805 *Prelude* 10: 935–40)

Here Wordsworth shows a terrible transformation. The sun of rational, enlightened inquiry that had seemed to light the world of the early revolution had been transformed into a "gewgaw, a machine" that "Sets like an opera phantom." Instead of becoming the source of renewed life and light and hope, the "sun" of rational thought has become a mechanical instrument that casts no real light on anything. The attempt to build social systems on reason alone has failed.

His initial solution to this quandary is instructive, because it is the solution that was mistakenly taken by his culture: instead of developing an epistemic model that could provide moral understanding, simply narrow the field of exploration until reason can serve its desired final function. He

> Yielded up moral questions in despair,
> And for my future studies, as the sole
> Employment of the inquiring faculty,
> Turned towards mathematics, and their clear
> And solid evidence. (1805 *Prelude* 10: 900–04)

Like his culture, Wordsworth's search for clarity and "truth" lead him to a point at which he is seduced by abstract reason and science. He amplifies this moment in the 1850 *Prelude*, where, in despair, he

> turned to abstract science, and there sought
> Work for the reasoning faculty enthroned
> Where the disturbances of space and time—
> Whether in matter's various properties
> Inherent, or from human will and power
> Derived—find no admission. (1850 *Prelude* 11: 328–33)

Rather than abandon the "enthroned" reasoning faculty, Wordsworth abandons moral questions. He seeks clarity and freedom from "the disturbances of space and time" in "abstract science."

This passage should have received more constructive attention as a dramatization than it has. Wordsworth clearly sets up an opposition here between moral questions and mathematics/abstract science, and shows that the clarity of one can be used as an escape from the complexity of the other. He speaks directly to the dominating intellectual forces of his time in this passage, and attacks in himself the tendency to rely on a model of knowledge that maintains the authority of reason only by reducing the scope of inquiry to the point at which it becomes trivial.

Wordsworth is "rescued" from this seduction, however, by two things: (1) his sister Dorothy, who spoke "in a voice / Of sudden admonition" and "preserved [him] still / a poet," and (2) "Nature's self" which "through the weary labyrinth / Conducted [him] again to open day" and "Gave [him] that strength and knowledge full of peace" (1805 *Prelude* 10: 909–925) that has upheld and still upholds him in the failure of the ideals of the French Revolution.

In the 1850 *Prelude*, he amplifies his antidote to the problem cited here, writing that

> Nature's self,
> By all varieties of human love
> Assisted, led me back through opening day
> To those sweet counsels between head and heart
> Whence grew that genuine knowledge, fraught with peace,
> Which, through the later sinkings of this cause,
> Hath still upheld me (1850 *Prelude* 11: 349–55)

He stresses the importance of grounding all reasonings in the language of real people, in the needs of real people, and in the contexts of personal experience, rather than allowing them to roam free in illusory worlds of categorizations and images without broader human value. He insists that participation and reflection are both required to come to value judgments. "Genuine knowledge" is not abstracted from moral issues, from human perceptions and feelings. It is, instead, a dialectic between "heart" and "head," between sympathetic identification and clear observation, between the individual and his or her environment and social situation. It is an ongoing process aimed at tuning and making harmony, rather than a system of definitive answers.

In this situation, as in many others throughout his poetry, Wordsworth is "admonished," reminded of larger processes than his own abstract reasoning, and regrounded. With scenes such as these, Wordsworth acknowledges the importance, and the shaping effects, of such "larger processes" as relationships, social responsibilities, and the universal order which is embodied in the landscape that surrounds him. John Rudy points out that

> Wordsworth's faith in his imagination, in his ability to form order out of potential chaos, is intimately conjoined with, indeed is inseparable from, his faith in the existence of orderly processes in the external world. ("Beyond Vocation" 641)

His interest in the self and the faculties of the human mind is always tempered by an awareness of the larger context within which the self and these faculties develop and must work. As Hewitt argues, he cannot be dismissed as an egotist simply because he "does not uphold abnegation of the self as an ideal" ("Faerie Lands" 68); it is his purpose to forge a meaningful relation between self and world, to allow "the 'ego' to function in relation to the rest of reality in which it is located" (68). His concept of reason reveals just such an awareness of the failure of the human mind to achieve anything of value when it is divorced from a firm grounding in the real world of experience, from a passionate connection with the world.

Wordsworthian Connections and Relationships

If, as Rudy claims in "Beyond Vocation," Wordsworth's faith in his own creative powers depends on his faith in the existence of orderly processes in the world around him, he must devote his attention to perceiving the orderliness and significance for human existence of these "larger processes." As Durrant asserts, "Wordsworth's poetry often reveals a strong interest in the structure of the physical universe as it had been re-defined by Newton and Boyle," and his poems "sometimes involve a rigorous considering of the conditions of human existence in such a universe" (18). How can man's complexity of feeling and creativity be reconciled with a mechanical world view? Even if such a view makes the larger processes surrounding the self "orderly," how does it accommodate any sort of meaningful relationship between self and world? Wordsworth does not beg these questions by simply dismissing the Newtonian vision of universal order and establishing a mystical and pantheistic view of nature. Instead, he attempts to transform the language and metaphors of Newtonian science from a set of abstract intellectual constructs into an emotionally charged, near-mythological view of a world that both influences and is influenced by the human mind.

Durrant argues that Wordsworth is an advocate of Newtonian science, and claims that "When Wordsworth condemns 'science' he almost always refers primarily to the moral 'science' of the age, and in particular to Godwinism" (3). But Durrant does not discuss the suggestive relationship between the science of Newton and its misapplication by thinkers such as Godwin—a relationship that illuminates Wordsworth's poetry. While Newton's synthesis is grand, it is fundamentally removed from human experience. Like geometry, it is true in a logical sense, but it still lacks "something of prime importance."

Durrant insists that the image of Newton offered in Book 3 of *The Prelude* reveals Wordsworth's veneration of the famous man of science. He writes that

> In this context, the enclosed, private, obscure life of the individual is lived in a confusion of business in which no clear pattern can be discerned; the life of the perceiving mind is set against this in the figure of Newton, whose grand synthesis of space and time is illustrated by the images of ordered time and of ordered space in the clock and the prism. (7)

In Durrant's opinion, Wordsworth was attracted to the "science which brought 'order and relation' into the world, and into the movements of the moon and stars" (7–8).

This passage, however, is more complex and ambiguous than Durrant makes it seem. Seen in the context of the passages that precede and follow it, it shows a respect for Newton and his great achievement which is tempered by an awareness of the abstraction and isolation that Newton's vision represents. Wordsworth sets Newton's statue in opposition to the "humming sound, less tuneable than bees / But hardly less industrious" (1805 *Prelude* 3: 48–49) of the kitchen underneath Wordsworth's rooms. Despite the "shrill notes / Of sharp command and scolding intermixed" (1805 *Prelude* 3: 49–50) the kitchens represent real life to Wordsworth; they are a focal point of human activity aimed at providing for the needs of "enjoying and suffering beings" (*1802 Pref, PW* 1: 141). The image of the clock is also active, moving, vital:

> Near me was Trinity's loquacious clock
> Who never let the quarters, night or day,
> Slip by him unproclaimed, and told the hours
> Twice over with a male and female voice.
> (1805 *Prelude* 3: 51–4)

The clock is nearly personified; it is "loquacious," telling its tale of time, alert and attentive to the events that surround it. Newton's statue, on the other hand, is represented by words that indicate loneliness and removal from human concerns. Wordsworth

> In moonlight nights
> Could see right opposite, a few yards off,
> The antechapel, where the statue stood
> Of Newton with his prism and silent face (1805 *Prelude* 3: 56–59)

With the moonlight, the silence, and the spatial orientation of Newton's statue "right opposite," Wordsworth associates Newton with the world of abstract and calculating thought to which the University aspires, a world of knowledge that is grand and powerful, but impersonal and unfeeling. He extends this feeling of "noble loneliness" further in the 1850 *Prelude* by adding lines describing Newton's statue as:

> The marble index of a mind for ever
> Voyaging through strange seas of Thought, alone. (*Prelude* 3: 59–63)

The impersonality of that world of knowledge is embodied in Wordsworth's remembrance of "important days, / Examinations, when the man was weighed / As in the balance." The young Wordsworth cannot feel comfortable here; he is disturbed by "a strangeness in the mind, / A feeling that I was not for that hour, / Nor for that place." With these words, Wordsworth begins a defense of his own pursuits in opposition to the accumulation of calculating knowledge that he doubts: a defense that cannot be fully articulated in his lifetime, but that, in its intuitive form, is central to his chosen path as a poet. He writes

> Why should I grieve?—I was a chosen son.
> For hither I had come with holy powers
> And faculties, whether to work or feel:
> To apprehend all passions and all moods
> Which time, and place, and season do impress
> Upon the visible universe, and work
> Like changes there by force of my own mind.
> (1805 *Prelude* 3: 82–8)

In this passage he states his epistemic difference: he is here to experience and shape the life around him—not simply to explain it or systematize it. He insists that he has within him a power of knowing that is different but not subordinate to the mode of intelligence offered by Cambridge and Newton. But how can he describe that knowledge, that mode of knowing, in the Cartesian language of his times? He can only sketch out an opposition between the world of the classroom that he deserts and the world of nature that he recovers when "As if with a rebound my mind returned / Into its former self." This moment, like the later crisis in Book 10/11, reveals an epistemic choice being made. Wordsworth chooses participation in natural processes, and embraces poetry as the form for communicating such participation. And he tries to explain these choices in terms that a Cartesian audience might understand.

By articulating complex ideas using recognizable terms and dichotomies, Wordsworth makes it easy for his readers to oversimplify those ideas. Here, for example, he seems to be rejecting "learning" as a whole. This kind of simplification has led to our view of Wordsworth as a "primitivist," an "unread poet of Nature," and so on. But we do not have to dichotomize. Even as he decides that Cambridge is not for him, Wordsworth does not condemn everything that it stands for. He does not simply embrace a "subjective" approach to life in opposition to the "objective" approach offered by Cambridge. He only knows that reason is not enough, that knowledge is not complete without participation in natural processes and imaginative engagement with the physical world.

In a letter to H.S. Tremenheere dated 16 December 1845, the mature Wordsworth speaks to this point in prose. He writes that

> We must not only have Knowledge but the means of wielding it, and that is done indefinitely more thro' the imaginative faculty assisting both in the collection and application of facts than is generally believed. (*LWW* 318)

Factual knowledge, he claims, is inert. We "wield" knowledge with the help of the "imaginative faculty" by engaging it, selecting and synthesizing it, and using it. The grand vision of Newton is not a meaningful addition to human knowledge unless we can engage it and put it to some moral use.

Wordsworth makes an attempt to do just that in the following passages. He reaches a state of connection with nature that refines Newton's vision—a state giving "a moral life" to all that it encounters, and linking the perceiving man to the largest and the smallest aspects of external nature. Wordsworth caps the passage with a vigorous statement wedding himself as a perceiver with all the forms of nature:

> I had an eye
> Which in my strongest workings evermore
> Was looking for the shades of difference
> As they lie hid in all exterior forms,
> Near or remote, minute or vast—an eye
> Which from a stone, a tree, a withered leaf,
> To the broad ocean and the azure heavens
> Spangled with kindred multitudes of stars,
> Could find no surface where its power might sleep,
> Which spake perpetual logic to my soul,
> And by an unrelenting agency
> Did bind my feelings even as in a chain.
> (1805 *Prelude* 3: 156–67)

This long passage represents the great wedding that Wordsworth attempts throughout his poetry. Here Wordsworth connects intellect and sympathy in a naturalized version of the Great Chain of Being, in which the self is linked to all aspects of the material world by a chain of "perpetual logic" and "feeling." Both aspects are vital; the relation is founded not just on intellectual questing, or on a vague "sympathy," but on a balanced use of the entire "comprehensive" mind. In this relationship, Wordsworth places the perceiver in a vital role. He is not the lonely thinker or "alienated observer" of science. She is not a "sole self" weaving false webs of imagination to comfort herself in an impersonal world. Instead, she is both a participant in the living processes of nature *and* a representer of those processes in language and image. This is the miracle that we are still struggling with even today. We are embedded in natural processes that we also can model and even change. Self-consciousness is not only a property of individuals, but of cultures.

The wedding of mind and world that Wordsworth proposes is non-linear. It is not two opposing forces that are yoked together, or one force (mind) yoked to a brute physical reality, or one force (mind) pitifully trying to claim that its own reality is *the* reality. Instead, it is a recursive joining of smaller and larger, or lower- and higher-level, living processes. The wedding represents Wordsworth's attempts to forge a middle path between transcendent and immanent philosophies by finding a link between material reality and states of experience (including the state of being conscious) that seem to transcend that palpable reality. I will discuss this tendency more fully in Chapter 5 when I explore Wordsworth's ecology of mind. But here, I will sketch out the central commitments of Wordsworth to (1) a comprehensive mind that encompasses participation and reflection, thinking and feeling, body and spirit and (2) imagination as a faculty that might join apparent opposites into a continuum of human experience.

The Comprehensive Mind

Wordsworth makes a dedicated attempt, in *The Prelude* and elsewhere, to ground human mental processes in the "real language of men" (*1802 Pref, PW* 1: 119), in concrete experiences of "Nature," and in application to the needs of real men and women. Yet he refuses to be confined by the determinism of Hartley's associationism, and places a high value on human creativity. *Imagination* becomes the concept that allows him to achieve both goals.

Wordsworth never defines imagination in clear, objective terms. Instead he treats it in terms of relationships and transactions. Far from dismissing reason and rationality, Wordsworth actually attempts to cast imagination in terms of reason itself. By the end of *The Prelude*, he states that imagination is "Reason in her most exalted mood" (1805 *Prelude* 13: 170), reason rooted in real experience (the "forms" of Nature) and emerging from and integrating human feelings. In Book 12, Wordsworth claims that

> Long time in search of knowledge desperate,
> I was benighted heart and mind, but now
> On all sides day began to reappear,
> And it was proved indeed that not in vain
> I had been taught to reverence a power
> That is the very quality and shape
> And image of right reason; (1805 *Prelude* 12: 20–26)

This "power" recalls his inchoate sense in Book 3 that he had come to Cambridge with "holy powers / And faculties, whether to work or feel," and anticipates his formulation of Imagination as "absolute power / And clearest insight, amplitude of mind, / And Reason in her most exalted mood" in Book 13/14. The words "very [later "visible"] quality," "shape," and "image" again firmly ground the power of Imagination in "Nature" and "the language of the sense." Wordsworth carefully avoids constructions of Imagination as an autonomous power of creation; instead, much to Coleridge's dismay, he allows that it is a mental process grounded in the biological structures of sensation and perception. But he does not relinquish the idea that it is a creative "power." How?

James Engell suggests that Imagination is a principle of relationship that is tantamount to love. Wordsworth agrees in *The Prelude* when he writes that "this love more intellectual cannot be / Without Imagination" (1805 *Prelude* 13: 188–9). Love is vital to any sense of human value or meaning; it connects us to each other and to nature. Wordsworth claims that

> From love, for here
> Do we begin and end, all grandeur comes
> All truth and beauty—from pervading love—
> That gone, we are as dust. (1805 *Prelude* 13: 149–52)

For Wordsworth, Imagination is like love because it is the central process that weds the "physical" and "mental" worlds that we inhabit. Imagination is literally the process of mental imaging. When it is harnessed to represent sensation, we call it perception. When it is harnessed to represent the feelings and situation of others, we call it sympathy. When it is harnessed to represent chains of thought, we call it reason. And when it is (un)harnessed to represent things that are not, or things that might be, or things that should be, we call it "creative imagination," dreaming or art. For Wordsworth, then, Imagination was the mental process that wedded "Nature"—or physical experience—and the Logos—or reality constructed mentally and symbolically.

With its combination of immanent and transcendent elements, "Tintern Abbey" typifies Wordsworth's vision of the recursive, complex wedding of the world of matter and motion and the world of thinking and purpose. He writes:

> ... I have felt
> A presence that disturbs me with the joy
> Of elevated thoughts, a sense sublime
> Of something far more deeply interfused,
> Whose dwelling is the light of setting suns,
> And the round ocean, and the living air,

> And the blue sky, and in the mind of man–
> A motion and a spirit that impels
> All thinking things, all objects of all thought,
> And rolls through all things. (*PoW* 110)

This passage evokes rather mechanical imagery—"motion," "impels," "objects," and "rolls"—to capture a spiritual feeling. Wordsworth insists that there is a direct connection between the moving world and "the mind of man," a connection of beauty and mysterious purpose. The connection is forged by imagination on several levels: perception and memory (which depend on both biological and intellectual representation), and higher-level symbolic representations, especially written and spoken language.

In the lines that follow, Wordsworth stresses this connection further with his famous formulation of "what we half-create / And perceive." He writes that he is

> —well pleased to recognize
> In Nature and the language of the sense
> The anchor of my purest thoughts, the nurse,
> The guide, the guardian of my heart, and soul
> Of all my moral being. (*PoW* 110)

This passage could be read as typical of Wordsworth's "peculiar faith in nature" which fails to "transcend science" (Bush 12). But it can just as easily be read as a Baconian statement of the importance of founding *all* of our ideas on empirical engagement rather than getting lost in chains of abstract reasoning. The words "anchor," "guide," and "guardian" all suggest such a reading. For Wordsworth, the "language of the sense" serves a triple function: it anchors his intellect, keeping his reason from becoming "sequestered"; it both inspires and contains his feelings and passions; and it serves as the very soul of his "moral being." If we as perceivers help to "half-create" the world of Nature, Nature also "half-creates" us and keeps us grounded in real experience. Wordsworth suggests this relation in his Preface to *Lyrical Ballads* when he claims that the poet "considers man and nature as essentially adapted to each other" (*1802 Pref, PW* 1: 140). He does not advocate an irrational worship of nature; in fact, he makes an empirical commitment that goes beyond that of most scientists.

It could be argued that the confusion about Wordsworth's religious views arises from this strange admixture of scientific empiricism and "spiritual" longing in his poetry. His imagery suggests an effort to forge an intellectual faith based on empirical rather than intuitive revelation, a faith grounded in biology rather than in "spirituality."[5] In a letter to Francis Wrangham (5 June 1808) he writes:

> I will allow with you that Religion is the eye of the Soul, but if we would have successful Soul-oculists, not merely that organ, but the general anatomy and constitution of the intellectual frame must be studied; farther, the powers of that eye are affected by the general state of the system. My meaning is, that piety and religion will be best understood by him who takes the most comprehensive view of the human mind, and that for the most part, they will strengthen with the general strength of the mind... (LWW 110)

In this letter, Wordsworth connects religious consciousness with intellectual power, and again uses the term "comprehensive" to describe the desirable state of human perception. Religious consciousness, like moral action, should arise from an active engagement of the mind with Nature.

With this poetic grounding, Wordsworth's claim that the Poet is "the rock of defence for human nature ... carrying everywhere with him relationship and love" (*1802 Pref, PW* 1: 141) makes perfect sense. The principle of relationship between self and world is expressed primarily in terms of "pleasure" in the Preface. Wordsworth makes it clear that "the pleasure which I have proposed to myself to impart, is of a kind very different from that which is supposed by many persons to be the proper object of poetry" (*1802 Pref, PW* 1: 131). He wishes to evoke pleasure in his readers, not for the sake of mere enjoyment, but for the sake of engaging them in a process of perception and thought and encouraging them to act. He connects pleasure with knowledge in a later passage, writing that

> We have no knowledge, that is, no general principles drawn from the contemplation of particular facts, but what has been built up by pleasure, and exists in us by pleasure alone. (*1802 Pref, PW* 1: 140)

These claims are broadened by application to the "Man of science, the Chemist and Mathematician" who also "know and feel this" (140). All knowing involves a willing engagement with the world, an engagement that arises from passionate interest and commitment.

Wordsworth then points out the difference between the types of knowledge offered by the "Poet" and the "Man of science," writing that

> The knowledge both of the Poet and the Man of science is pleasure; but the knowledge of the one cleaves to us as a necessary part of our existence, our natural and unalienable inheritance; the other is a personal and individual acquisition, slow to come to us, and by no habitual and direct sympathy connecting us with our fellow-beings. The Man of science seeks truth as a remote and unknown benefactor; he cherishes and loves it in his solitude: the Poet, singing a song in which all human beings join with him, rejoices in the presence of truth as our visible friend and hourly companion. (*1802 Pref, PW* 1: 140–41)

It is vital to note the language here: science is associated with the "remote", with "solitude", with the "unknown"; it is disassociated from "connection" and "sympathy." Poetry, on the other hand, is associated with the "natural", with a "song" in which "all human beings join"; it is a "visible friend and hourly companion". It is also interesting to note that Science is considered "personal" and "individual" while poetry is considered "universal." Wordsworth turns some common conceptions on their heads here; the scientist is more likely to be an egotist, removed from the concerns that unite all men as "enjoying and suffering beings" (*1802 Pref, PW* 1: 141). The poet is involved in the ongoing effort to make connections, to bring "relationship and love" to the world.

With this in mind, it seems quite unfair to accuse Wordsworth of being "egotistical," of using his imagination to appropriate everything to himself, to control reality and internalize it for his own isolated use. It seems much more likely that he employed his personal experience, which is the only source of valid knowledge for an empirical thinker, in an effort to establish a meaningful relationship between the human self and the Newtonian world. Rudy's claim that the memorial poems "employ the imagination as a vital participant in various shaping processes rather than as a potentially apocalyptic energy servicing the needs and expectations of a separate, bifurcating self" ("Beyond Vocation" 638) can be applied to most of Wordsworth's poetry. In *The Borderers*, at the moment when Mortimer/Marmaduke is preparing to kill Herbert in the dungeon, he looks up and "beheld a star twinkling over my head , and by the living God, [he] could not do it" (*Borderers* 168).

Wordsworth calls upon such sudden connections with larger processes over and over in his poetry as a corrective to the isolation of the "self as mind" (Rzepka). Wordsworth attempts to wed the individual "feeling intellect" to the world of "larger processes" in a spiraling development of the self in relation to that world. This process of development and refinement becomes for him a scientific (or empirical) foundation for his "religious" beliefs and inspiration. For him the self is a comprehending thing which in order to grow must also be comprehensive—it must forever return to engagement with people, with nature, and with the world around it. And that continual re-engagement requires a model of knowing very different from the hierarchical, linear models of philosophy and science. Wordsworth's compositions offer a history of his struggle to generate and apply such a model—a struggle that can be seen in its inception in the fragment called "Essay on Morals."

Chapter 4
Constructing a Rhetorical Epistemology

> Nothing has meaning except it be seen as in some context.
> —Gregory Bateson, *Mind and Nature*

At the very beginning of his career, Wordsworth made statements that centered on the issues of individual perception, feeling, and the contexts in which humans come to know. These statements went against the intellectual grain of his time, which valued universal "truths," thinking, and the context-free formulations of clear analytical systems for understanding phenomena. That Wordsworth felt a desire for a "system" that placed individuals into a coherent relationship with the world cannot be argued. He shows his desire for unity and comprehensive meaning in everything he writes. Yet, as mentioned in the previous chapter, he felt that "something of prime importance was missing" in intellectual systems. That "something" had to do with moral value and action, but it also had to do with the very nature of systems themselves. Wordsworth felt that abstract propositions about reality or ethics or morals were powerless unless they (1) clearly emerged from and informed particular contexts, and (2) remained in vital contact with, and subject to revision by, those contexts. He indicated very early in his writing that systems as they were being constructed in his time relied far too heavily on abstract propositions and left human contexts for understanding and applying principles behind.

As early as the fragment "Essay on Morals," Wordsworth shows his concern with the development of context-free intellectual "systems" of behavior and meaning. The very first sentence creates a conundrum:

> I THINK publications in which we formally & systematically lay down rules for the actions of Men cannot be too long delayed. (*EoM, PW* 1: 103)

Wordsworth's ambivalence about "systems" is embedded in this statement. Does he mean that systematic publications better than the ones already available (Godwin, Paley, and others) must surely arrive on the scene soon ("cannot be too long delayed")? Or does he mean that such publications cannot be delayed long enough, because even when they are published they are inadequate to the task that they set for themselves and create more problems than they resolve? Either reading can be seen as consistent with Wordsworth's ensuing attack on the philosophical systems of Godwin and Paley, but the difference between the two possible readings—and its potential significance—requires us to be careful as we account for Wordsworth's view of intellectual systems.

Wordsworth's ambivalence concerning systems here and elsewhere is interesting and informative. It emerges from his conflicting sense that, on the one hand, the universe is orderly and meaningful, yet on the other hand, "systems of moral philosophy" do not do a very complete or comprehensive job of describing, explaining or furthering that order. In the Preface to *Lyrical Ballads*, for example, he refuses to undertake a "systematic defence of the theory, upon which the poems were written" (*1800 Pref, PW* 1: 120) for two reasons. First, he claims that such systematic arguments would be unconvincing to his readers:

> on this occasion the Reader would look coldly upon my arguments, since I might be suspected of having been principally influenced by the selfish and foolish hope of reasoning him into an approbation of these particular poems (*1800 Pref, PW* 1: 120).

And second, he claims that the connected issues to be explored would simply be too vast for coverage in the Preface. In order to defend his poetry fairly and completely, he says,

> it would be necessary to give a full account of the present state of the public taste in this country, and to determine how far this taste is healthy or depraved; which, again, could not be determined, without pointing out in what manner language and the human mind act and re-act on each other, and without tracing the revolutions, not of literature alone, but likewise of society itself (*1800 Pref, PW* 1: 120).

In this sweeping statement, Wordsworth vitally connects human psychology, both of creation ("in what manner language and the human mind re-act on each other") and reception ("taste"), with "literary theory" ("revolutions" of "literature") and history and political theory ("revolutions" of "society itself"). And he does so because he sees all these things as fundamentally connected.

These two threads provide insight into the things that worry Wordsworth about systematic approaches to reality. He senses that immediate experience (reading the poems, in this case) influences a human being far more than any talking about experience ("reasoning" about why they are worth reading). If his poems did not move his readers on their own merits, he saw no hope of convincing them to be moved. Systems lose power to move because they focus on explanations of experience, rather than experience itself. Or, let us say, the experience of reading about abstract systems of thought is not as moving or powerful as the experience of reading about people and actions with which we can identify ourselves.

Wordsworth also suggests the complexity of connections involved in thinking about the way the mind, and language, work in poetry. One cannot limit oneself to a discussion of "poetic language"; one must include circuitous paths of influence—mind acting and reacting with the world through perception, mind acting and reacting with other minds through language, cultural predispositions and the way they shape and limit these other processes. Wordsworth's description of the task does not seem to lend itself to linear, logical, systematic analysis.

Yet Wordsworth does not refuse the idea that such a systematic view could be constructed. In the Preface, his remarks about the complexity of describing poetry begin with an acknowledgment that he believes the subject to be "susceptible" to clear and coherent treatment (*1800 Pref, PW* 1: 120). This acknowledgment suggests that the subject *could* be treated systematically if he had the time and space to do so. And later in the Preface, he cites his belief that "a time is approaching when the evil will be systematically opposed by men of greater powers and with far more distinguished success" (*1800 Pref, PW* 1: 130).[1]

This division, or ambivalence, in Wordsworth's view of systems, can be attributed to his desire to construct an orderly view of the world that was not reductive. He sought a system that remained in touch with the complexities of human relationship, with the world of "Flesh & Blood." The two issues—the failure of systematic, rational thinking to *move* people, and the failure of such thinking to account for complex and circuitous relationships—are central issues in Wordsworth's compositions. And he considers them rigorously. Even as Wordsworth rejects "systematic thinking," he insists on "long intercourse" and focused engagement. Even as he stresses individual perception, he insists that perception occurs within, and is corrected by, larger natural and social processes. While his approach is not "systematic," it is disciplined.

In *Making Tales*, Bialostosky recognizes Wordsworth's disciplined intellectual force but articulates it as a desire for poetry to be taken seriously in "systematic" terms:

> Even those who have not fallen back upon the fated taste of their age or Wordsworth's and have acknowledged the "immense demands" which Wordsworth's poetry makes upon its readers rarely see that *Wordsworth's most important demand is for the active study of poetry as a systematic discipline* [emphasis mine]. (7)

While the impulse behind the highlighted pronouncement is correct, the terms, as Bialostosky uses them, are dangerous to our understanding of Wordsworth. "Study" implies the Cartesian divide between subject and object; to "study" poetry we must first place it at arm's length and then analyze it from that carefully constructed distance. "Systematic" and "discipline" both imply the philosophical modes of knowing established by Aristotle's vast scheme of categorizing and subdividing all experience and all knowledge.

Wordsworth's discussions of poetry refuse these implications. He is much more concerned that the reader "enter into the spirit" of the poems by participating in them fully.[2] The only way one can learn to enjoy the poems is to engage them as experiences (not as artificial objects for "study"). Bialostosky errs by using terminology that enmeshes him in the Cartesian/Philosophical mode— the very mode that Wordsworth was so anxious to disrupt by offering his experimental alternatives.

To turn the terminology to better effect, let us remove "systematic" and "study" completely, because both connote fixed categories and final pronouncements. Now let's turn "discipline" to a new and better use. Instead of using it as a "category-noun," let's use it as an adjective describing "engagement"—a word that comes much closer to Wordsworth's view of the reader's involvement with poetic experience. Let's keep "active," because it is a central descriptor that rings true. Now we have something like this:

> Wordsworth's most important demand is for the active and disciplined engagement of poetry.

I believe that this is a better reading of Wordsworth's compositions. It summarizes his insistence that the reader should leave behind "pre-established codes of decision," and that readers should be patient and should try to learn to experience the poetry before dismissing it (*Adv*, *PW* 1: 116–17). Wordsworth encourages his readers to judge his compositions, but only after they have participated in them fully and well.

John Nabholtz claims that the Preface should be understood as a rhetorical work rather than as "systematic" literary theory, and asserts that

> In the "Preface," Wordsworth *as writer* was primarily concerned with *creating a favorably disposed and activated reader*... (80)

His argument is quite sound, but it leaves the problem of literary and other theories—knowledge—out of the picture. This would have been an unacceptable omission for Wordsworth. My argument is that Wordsworth connected literary theory and creative theory and rhetoric into an epistemological continuum. Wordsworth's insistence on "active and disciplined engagement" represents a rhetorical stance that underlies his discourse experiments, and it is, fundamentally, an epistemic rhetorical stance. Knowing is a creative process that takes place by way of active, disciplined, and ongoing engagement with other minds, with communities, and with the natural world. It is always a tentative process in which minds grope for connections and generate possible meanings in the process of shaping an opinion, a judgment, or a belief. Discourse that purports to impart knowledge, then, is always experimental—both in its exploration of ways of reaching readers and in its exploration of ideas and subjects.

Wordsworth's Principles of Knowing: Perception, Representation and Considered Experience

> These bald & naked reasonings are impotent over our habits, they cannot form them; from the same cause they are equally powerless in regulating our judgments concerning the value of men & things. They contain no picture of human life;

they describe nothing. (*EoM, PW* 1: 103)

"The principal object, then, proposed in these Poems was to choose incidents and situations from common life, and to relate or describe them, throughout, as far as was possible in a selection of language really used by men, and, at the same time, to throw over them a certain colouring of imagination, whereby ordinary things should be presented to the mind in an unusual aspect ..." (*1802 Pref, PW* 1: 123)

Wordsworth shows in these two passages his commitment to the empirical idea that our knowledge of the world begins with particular experiences: an event, a meeting with a person, a feeling about something that happens to us. In many cases, the particular experience is forgotten almost immediately. We never represent it to ourselves as significant, and so it disappears into the backwash of our perceptual data. Often, however, we pay enough attention to make the experience available, at least in outline, for us to recall to our mind's eye (memory) for some time. And sometimes our attention is so keen, and our representation of the event to ourselves so strong, that the particular event may transform our view of who we are and what is important to us.

In addition to our particular experiences, we also conceive of our experiences in general terms, developing classes of experiences and developing value expectations that are aligned with those classes. Our classing of experiences often becomes, like it or not, a filter for new experiences—a way of immediately assigning value and meaning to the experience of the moment. Our symbolic construction of the world—our personal logos—begins to harden, and to exclude new experiences. We develop a set of habits of mind, ways of engaging experience, that are not easy to change with simple conscious adjustment. Even so, a striking personal experience can sometimes carry enough authority to overcome our constructions, and to force us to reconsider those constructions.

But other people have different experiences, and their experiences may lead them to different sets of generalized "rules." How much weight do their generalizations carry with us? Not much, unless we share enough of the primary experiences on which those generalizations are based to pay close attention to them and to learn to value them. And what about generalized systems based on the experience of many people? These systems are developed at a higher level of abstraction, and are even further removed from the domain of personal experience that moves the individual.

Wordsworth's argument against Godwin and Paley in the "Essay on Morals" was based on an intuitive understanding of these levels of abstraction. In this little document, he asserts the failure of systematic, generalized reasoning to change deeply ingrained "habits of mind." Something must be experienced *immediately*—felt on the pulses, to borrow Keats' phrase—in order to effect change. Wordsworth writes:

> Can it be imagined by any man who has deeply examined his own heart that an old habit will be foregone, or a new one formed, by a series of propositions, which, presenting no image to the [? mind] can convey no feeling which has any connection with the supposed archetype or fountain of the proposition existing in human life? (*EoM, PW* 1: 103)

This passage is critical to understanding Wordsworth, because it helps us to understand what he means by "feeling"—a word that he relies on heavily in the Prefaces. Feeling is a mental state that is associated with perception rather than with reasoning. It emerges from experience—"the supposed archetype or fountain of the proposition existing in human life"—and not from abstractions of thought—"a series of propositions." Our feelings may make us shun or ignore some situations while welcoming others. In short, feeling is vital to the process of placing a value on experience—to meaning-making. To address reason directly with abstract propositions is pointless. Unless those propositions are grounded in a real-life context, and effectively address the feelings of the audience, they can have little or no effect on the audience's habits of thinking and making decisions.

Wordsworth continues along these lines, writing that

> These moralists attempt to strip the mind of all its old clothing when their object ought to be to furnish it with new. All this is the consequence of an undue value set upon that faculty which we call reason. The whole secret of this juggler's trick[?s] lies (not in fitting words to things (which would be a noble employment) but) in fitting things to words. (*EoM, PW* 1: 103)

He makes several significant claims here. First, he asserts that the aim of the moralist must be to furnish the reader with new habits of mind (rather than simply tearing up their old habits). Second, he asserts that we must not overvalue or rely too much on "reason" in this process, because it is a verbal and conceptual "juggler" rather than a source of images and feelings that can produce real change. And he implies that while reason focuses on "fitting things to words," the noble employment in this case would be "fitting words to things." This distinction sounds tautological, but it really isn't. It comes from Wordsworth's understanding of the importance of representation in our thinking processes, and from his awareness that as we develop a body of experience, we also develop "pre-established codes of decision" (*Adv*, *PW* 1: 116) that limit our ways of engaging new experiences. To "fit things to words" is to make new experiences fit existing concepts and terms. On the other hand, to "fit words to things" implies being true to new perceptions and trying to somehow capture them in all their complexity with the limited language that we have available. I believe wholeheartedly that Wordsworth saw himself, and all true Poets, as participants in this "noble employment."

The four points raised by Wordsworth in the "Essay on Morals" provide an excellent starting point for an exploration of Wordsworth's model of knowing and the ways in which it provides a context for his discourse experiments. These points, in summary, are as follows:

1. Abstract reasonings are essentially powerless to move us; as individuals grounded in perception, we can only be moved by particular experiences, particular images, and concrete events. To be affective/effective, reasoning must always emerge from, and return to, those experiences, images, and events.
2. Systematic thinking (concepts to be applied in all contexts) is not adequate to the task of moral knowing. Nevertheless, it is possible and desirable to develop unified structures of knowledge rather than confining knowledge to the context of each individual in his/her personal life.
3. The processes of mind are best understood not in terms of "Reason" but in terms of evolving "Habits." Reasoning always takes place within a mental context that is framed by the habits of mind we have developed over time. Our primary aim as learners/knowers is to develop and "tune" our habits of mind.
4. Language represents experience. As such, it can either place new experiences into existing categories or it can attempt to stretch itself into the shape of new experience. The first approach emphasizes clarity of language even at the expense of

reducing perceptual complexities to a false simplicity; the second emphasizes the effort to represent perceptual complexities well, even if that leads to contradictory and complicated uses of language (paradox, redefinition, and so on). While the former provides security and closure, the latter is the more "noble employment."

These four points set forth several important principles of what can be considered a "rhetorical epistemology" that informs the body of Wordsworth's composition. They place language and representation at the center of our processes of knowing, and they place a higher priority on experiential processes than on the products of reasoning. They also imply that the knower, whether poet or audience, must be engaged, open-minded, and ready to participate in order for knowing to take place. While these ideas do not represent Wordsworth's "model of knowing" completely or finally, they do inform the body of his work in significant ways. For the purposes of this inquiry, then, the four principles outlined here will be considered as the central threads upon which the web of Wordsworth's discourse experiments is spun. The web is made of imagination, or mental images, and its pattern emerges from *physical and mental representation*—the unconsciously-produced "images" and "forms" of sensual experience and the consciously-and unconsciously-produced "images" and "forms" of art.

But it is also possible, and in a text of this nature desirable, to view such a web step-by-step—to examine its structure in linear terms. The remainder of this text will be divided into four chapters that examine and expand on the four principles outlined above. The next chapter will discuss Wordsworth's effort to ground knowing in personal experience and individual perception rather than in "clear and distinct" mental models that were already in place. It will argue that Wordsworth viewed disciplined and "open" perception, and ongoing engagement and participation in new experiences, as the necessary point of origin for valuable conceptions and mental models.

The following two chapters address the issues of "larger processes" and "habits of mind" as correctives for the potential "subjectivity" of the individual knower. The first asserts that Wordsworth was striving to articulate an ecology of mind like the one that Gregory Bateson suggests in his work—a view in which human minds are connected within, and constituted by, larger mind-like processes of family, social structure, and the natural world. He asserts that if we open our perception to such larger processes, reflect on them, and "tune" ourselves with them, our habits of feeling, thinking, and acting will be improved. The second discusses the development of good habits of mind within the context of classical rhetoric, and shows the way that good representation and attention to habits of mind can also serve as a "corrective" to "subjective knowing." This chapter will also reconstruct a view of knowing in which rhetoric and representation play central roles.

The final chapter then recontextualizes, within Wordsworth's view of knowing, the nature of poetry and the poet's role as he describes and practices them in the *Lyrical Ballads*. The issues of language raised in the "Essay on Morals" are revisited within the context of the poetry and shown in praxis.

Wordsworth's Alternative Model of Knowing

...both thought and thing are forms abstracted from the total process.
—David Bohm, *Wholeness and the Implicate Order*

Modern science and technology are based not only on a hostile attitude toward the environment, but on the repression of the body and the unconscious; and unless these can be recovered, unless participating consciousness can be restored in a way that is scientifically (or at least rationally) credible and not merely a relapse into naïve animism, then what it means to be a human being will be forever lost.
—Morris Berman, *The Reenchantment of the World*

I hold to the presupposition that our loss of the sense of aesthetic unity was, quite simply, an epistemological mistake. I believe that that mistake may be more serious than all the minor insanities that characterize those older epistemologies which agreed upon the fundamental unity.
—Gregory Bateson, *Mind and Nature*

Chapter 5
Perception and Participation

Wordsworth's interest in perception, particularly his own, is well documented. But Cartesian dualism has relegated his writings about perception to the realm of the "subjective" or the "expressive"—the utterances of an individual whose perceptions could have no real authority for any other mind. In fact, his stress on individual perception has often been read as a rejection of reasonable, factually-grounded thinking in favor of personal interpretation. That reading emerges from the philosophical inclination to free knowledge from its inevitably personal origins and uses. What is often lost in the effort to forge "objective" knowledge is an examination of the implications of a very simple empirical fact that Bateson states with no equivocation in *Mind and Nature*: "all experience is subjective" (31). We perceive images that are produced unconsciously according to rules that we cannot easily change, and "objective reality," if there is such a thing, is not the same thing as our perceptions of it. Bateson accepts that fact as the basis of epistemology and develops a worldview in which it does not cripple science or devalue knowing. But in Wordsworth's time, this fact of empirical thinking, when pursued into the domain of philosophical inquiry, led to a dilemma of unprecedented proportions.

Descartes' writings, and the theories of mental process—loosely grouped under the term "associationism"—that were being discussed in the eighteenth century, both place perception in the mechanical role of simply mirroring "reality" in the mind. If all perception is subjective, we must rely on a pre-existing "reality" to give our perceptions a "ground" of accuracy and truth. And that means that individual differences in perception become either (1) the result of affective differences or personal abnormalities that have nothing to do with real knowledge, which is clearly apparent to those who perceive the world more clearly and distinctly, or (2) incredibly threatening, because they suggest that "reality" may not be accessible to us, and that we have no basis for believing in a shared and sharable world of mental images at all. In general, empirical philosophers relied on a pre-existing reality to ground their systems[1] and rationalists and idealists relied on God (rather unconvincingly).2

Regina Hewitt's book *Wordsworth and the Empirical Dilemma* provides a nice background on the problem of perception for empirical thinkers, and places Wordsworth in a unique position with regard to the "Empirical Dilemma." She states, quite accurately, that

> Wordsworth begins by accepting the individuality of all perception that his contemporaries wished to circumvent. He then explores how writers and readers can take advantage of this condition if they abandon their pursuit of a chimerical consensus and channel their efforts into the creation of functional relationships. (33)

This claim helps to reunite Wordsworth's stress on individual perception—his own, particularly—and his claims that his poetry had important social and moral purposes. As classical rhetoricians knew, we human beings represent reality to ourselves somehow, and we choose courses of action on the basis of our representations. Wordsworth's interest lies in the processes of biological and linguistic representation, and the all-important role of representation in the making of meaning.

That interest places him in the company of many of the most advanced thinkers of the twentieth century: psychologists, language theorists, neurologists, anthropologists, and physical scientists. Wordsworth's beliefs that mind and nature are connected, that perception is of supreme importance in the process of knowing, and that personal experience is therefore the matrix on which knowledge is always built, are no longer considered "mystical." Scientists are now beginning to take seriously the importance of perception and consciousness in the construction of "reality." Physicist David Darling writes that

> the conscious mind is crucially involved in establishing what is real. That which reaches our senses is, at best, a confusion of phantasmal energies— not sights, or sounds, or any of the coherent qualities that we project outward onto the physical world. The universe, as we know it, is built and experienced entirely within our heads, and until that mental construction takes place, reality must wait in the wings. (103–4)

Physicist David Bohm has made similar claims, claims that are uncomfortably close to this one:

> the world of everyday life is not real, or out there, as we believe it is ... reality, or the world we all know, is only a description. (in Castaneda viii)

Strangely enough, the new physics lends itself to a complete agreement with Castaneda's mysterious Yaqui Indian sorcerer. Many well-respected physicists now believe, like don Juan, that there is no describable "reality" without some perceiver to assemble or organize it.

And yet we live within these descriptions—what Chandler would call "Second Nature"—and treat them as if they were "Nature" itself. Wordsworth's awareness of this condition, and his sense that it is a problem, is evidenced by a passage from the *Two-Part Prelude* and its evolution through the 1805 and 1850 revisions of the *Prelude*. In this passage, Wordsworth addresses Coleridge, originally writing:

> Thou, my friend, art one
> More deeply read in thy own thoughts, no slave
> Of that false secondary power by which
> In weakness we create distinctions, then
> Believe our puny boundaries are things
> Which we perceive, and not which we have made.
> (*Two-Part Prelude* 2: 249–54)

Whether "that false secondary power" is "reason" or some other faculty, this passage shows considerable insight—especially for the early nineteenth century—into the way that language structures and mental models can influence perception.

In the 1805 version, Wordsworth extends the 1799 passage to focus on the role that science, in particular, plays in this problem of perception:

> Thou, my friend, art one
> More deeply read in thy own thoughts; ***to thee***
> ***Science appears but what in truth she is,***
> ***Not as our glory and our absolute boast,***
> ***But as a succedaneum, and a prop***
> ***To our infirmity.*** [emphasis mine] Thou art no slave
> Of that false secondary power by which
> In weakness we create distinctions, then
> Deem that our puny boundaries are things
> Which we perceive, and not which we have made.
> (1805 *Prelude* 2: 215–224)

This language is misread in Wordsworth, Abrams, and Gill's edition of the 1799, 1805, and 1850 *Preludes*. The word *succedaneum*, they claim, means "remedy"—and "this is a misuse of the word." In fact, *succedaneum* means "substitute" from the Latin *succedere* "to follow after." And that is precisely what Wordsworth means. Abstract learning always follows after, and attempts to explain, our perceptual experiences. And we tend to build a world of categories and labels that we then "substitute" for the world of experiences itself.

Wordsworth, Abrams, and Gill claim that the meaning of "science" here is "learning" in the generic sense, but the contexts we have developed demand the other, more specific meanings of the word available to Wordsworth in the 1790s. The *Oxford English Dictionary* states that the word "science" indicates "demonstrable knowledge" as opposed to "belief" or "opinion"; in addition, it tends to refer to "observed facts systematically classified" and "general laws." All in all, Wordsworth used the term to indicate the narrowly-focused, systematic, abstract knowledge typical of the physical and natural "sciences" of his day.

He takes this a step further in the 1850 *Prelude* when he completes the passage with:

> No officious slave
> Art thou of that false secondary power
> By which we multiply distinctions, then
> Deem that our puny boundaries are things
> That we perceive, and not that we have made.
> (1850 *Prelude* 2: 215–19)

This passage is truer to the sense he is aiming for. Rather than allowing that "science" *creates* distinctions, he now claims that science simply "multiplies" distinctions by subdividing knowledge into smaller and smaller categories (echoing the famous "murder to dissect" idea). He also amplifies the term "slave" by adding "officious" ("dutiful" or "obliging" or "meddlesome")—implying that many people are more than willing to live in the world of abstractions and to attempt to force them down our throats.

This passage, in all its evolving forms, emerges from the conviction that humans can, and do, tend to perceive the world through the lens of "pre-established codes of decision" and ready-made categories. But perhaps, as Wordsworth suggests, it is possible to discipline ourselves in ways that help us to perceive better—to return to perception without all the baggage of categorizations and pre-conceived notions. A significant part of his poetic enterprise centered on educating, and attempting to engage, *perception*, which was the part of knowing that had typically been assumed (mirroring reality) or uneasily avoided as a central component in theories of knowing.

The Complexities of Perception

Wordsworth spends a great deal of his poetic time exploring the ways in which his own perceptions were educated, the ways in which his mind developed in contact with "Nature." He comes to the conclusion in his developing *Prelude* and in "Tintern Abbey" that there are in fact two "consciousnesses" and two "worlds." The first consciousness is immediate participation in experience—the vital sense of belonging in and to the natural world that he felt as a boy. The second is reflective consciousness, which no longer feels so enraptured by nature but which can still perceive and value its beauty and power. And while he often regrets the "loss" of the former consciousness, and attempts to recapture it, he does not deny the value of the latter consciousness.

The two worlds are cited in the prior passage from *The Two-Part Prelude*. One world is the world of what Wordsworth calls "Nature"—of perceptual experience prior to our descriptions and explanations and mental models. The second world can be labeled "Second Nature" (as Chandler has used the term, with some extension)—the world of mental models consisting of traditions, customs, pre-existing codes of decision and intellectual "systems."

A good epistemology must recognize and deal effectively with the "two consciousness/two world" problem. The greatest epistemological error lies in what Bateson has called "map containment"—mistaking the models or maps that we make for the territory we are modeling or mapping. And "scientific epistemology," by treating perception and language as "transparent" and denying the role of the individual perceiver in the symbolic construction of meaning, has built its entire edifice of knowledge on this very error.

As Berman claims, both the rationalist and empirical traditions have centered on the world of mental models. In these traditions, knowledge *is* the mental models themselves; experience is only a means to get and use knowledge. Mysticism, on the other hand, suggests that mental models are never accurate and that we must let go of them entirely in order to escape the tyranny of ideas. Wordsworth's critique of systems in the "Essay on Morals," and his articulated principles of knowing in the Prefaces, offer a third approach to the two worlds/two consciousnesses problem. They stress the process of moving between the two worlds as central to knowing, and suggest that knowing can be refined and made valuable by developing better mental processes.

Two Worlds, Two Consciousnesses: Relationship-Centered Epistemology

Wordsworth's view of two worlds and two consciousnesses seems to anticipate the complexities of language and thought raised in recent years by poststructural thinkers. Yet he never accepted the idea that we completely lose the world of immediate perception upon our acquisition of language, customs, and conceptual frameworks. Newtonian science treated the physical world as a designed object that existed "outside" and in which the individual consciousness had no sacred place. Poststructural thinking treats the physical world as practically inaccessible to individual consciousness, which is formed linguistically by cultural constructs of concept, custom, and tradition. Both positions create devastating traps for the individual consciousness by positing an external world of either physical reality or "textuality" that isolates and controls the "subject" completely.

Wordsworth's use of Nature as a construct separate from Second Nature (the accumulated set of concepts, traditions, and customs which frames individual experiences) is richer than critics have allowed. Arnold read it as a form of escapism, and many have used it as such. Thomas Pfau sees it in poststructural terms as an attempt to recover an "objective field of reference" for the "poetic sign"—again returning to Cartesian dualism by suggesting that Wordsworth was setting up a different textual world in opposition to the textual world of London. But if Nature is seen as the world of immediate perception prior to conceptualization—admittedly an idealization, but a pointer to aid understanding—then Wordsworth's thrust makes better sense.

Wordsworth saw that human beings responded to the world habitually, in modes that were bound by the constraints of language, custom, and tradition as well as by predispositions shaped by personal experience. In order to talk about the problems of Second Nature (the veil that stands between our perception and the world to be perceived— the 'thousand things' that stand between a historian or a biographer and his/her subject (*1802 Pref*, *PW* 1: 139)), he had to first imagine a position in which Second Nature plays no part. Wordsworth certainly created Nature as a field of reference in opposition to the artificiality of city life and city tastes that he implied were "depraved." But he might also have posited Nature as a corrective for the rational systems of thought addressed in the "Essay on Morals"—systems that he claimed stood outside of, and out of touch with, immediate perception and sensation. And he may also have posited Nature and the 'return to nature' as counterbalances for the customary predisposition of the individual to dismiss things that have been culturally labeled as "unimportant" before sensing or engaging them fully. In any case, Second Nature can be seen as a model of experience that is no longer in touch with the process of engaging experience itself. It is the "map"—a shell which surrounds experience and which we treat as if it were experience.

But, since language itself is a part of Second Nature (as Wordsworth states so firmly concerning the artificiality of the "Poetic Diction" of the late eighteenth century), he found himself in a difficult position when attempting to combat the problem. In the 1802 Preface to Lyrical ballads, for example, he makes a distinction between the Poet's "employment," which "is in some degree mechanical," and the "freedom and power of real and substantial action and suffering" (*PW* 1: 138). As a rule, Wordsworth understands that speaking about events is not as powerful or meaningful as participating in them. And so he suggests that only through intense participation can the speaking gain any authority and power:

> ... it will be the wish of the Poet to bring his feelings near to those of the persons whose feelings he describes, nay, for short spaces of time, perhaps, to let himself slip into an entire delusion, and even confound and identify his own feelings with theirs; modifying only the language which is thus suggested to him by a consideration that he describes for a particular purpose, that of giving pleasure. (*PW* 1: 138)

What he describes here is entry into "participating consciousness." The Poet must enter the world of his subject, must experience it, and must attempt to convey that experience powerfully in language. The language should emerge from the experience, rather than simply being applied to it. Once again, we see the distinction that Wordsworth makes in the "Essay on Morals" between "fitting words to things" and "fitting things to words." When an individual is trapped in Second Nature, he uses language as if it were the final authority. When an individual returns to Nature, she uses language tenuously—always aware that the experience itself is primary and the language used to describe it is secondary. The former use of language is systematic and rule-bound, the latter is always embedded in, and emerging from, particular contexts.

In a sense, Second Nature of all sorts is a result of habits—of thinking, perceiving, and acting. Wordsworth sought to come up with a way of reshaping—rather than eradicating—those habits. In order to do so, he settled on views of

1. Nature as perceived world rather than as conceptual world. This immediately places him in an entirely different domain from Newton, and it immediately places the individual at the center of Wordsworth's vision.
2. Perception as the "language of the sense"—the "images" and "forms" discussed so effectively by Clarke which provided the point of relationship between the individual mind and Nature.
3. 'Natural language' as language that emerges from "fitting words to things" rather than "fitting things to words." This distinction, though poorly developed by Wordsworth, served several purposes:
    (A) attempting to make language convey the perceived complications of relationships instead of the conceived simplicity of "things."
    (B) becoming a source of identification with the reader by placing the images first and the language itself second.

Disciplining Perception

Perceptual experience, rather than conceptual models of experience, was the ground to which Wordsworth continually returned. And to be effective at conveying his own experience to others, he had to encourage immediate perception and participation in his writing. He had to move his readers away from "pre-established codes of decision" and toward complete involvement of the sort that he described as necessary to the Poet describing his subjects. As early as the 1798 Advertisement to *Lyrical Ballads*, Wordsworth calls on the authority of the *reader's experience* of the poems, and not on the authority of pre-existing poetic standards or the stylistic perfections of the poems themselves.

> readers, for their own sakes, should not suffer the solitary word Poetry ... to stand in the way of their gratification; ... they should ask themselves if it [this book] contains a natural delineation of human passions, human characters, and human incidents ... (*PW* 1: 116)

The discipline necessary for developing an "accurate taste in poetry," Wordsworth claims, has little to do with learning the categories and codes of "Poetry." Instead it requires a willing engagement of unfamiliar experiences and a willingness to re-examine one's "pre-established codes of decision" in the light of those new experiences:

> An accurate taste in Poetry, and in all the other arts, Sir Joshua Reynolds has observed, is an acquired talent, which can only be produced by severe thought, and a long continued intercourse with the best models of composition. This is mentioned not with so ridiculous a purpose as to prevent the most inexperienced reader from judging for himself; but merely to temper the rashness of decision, and to suggest that if poetry be a subject on which much time has not been bestowed, the judgment may be erroneous, and that in many cases it necessarily will be so. (*Adv, PW* 1: 116–17)

This passage sets forth the reader as the judge, but asserts that the reader's transactions with the text must become "self-correcting." To react on the basis of first impressions is not adequate; repeated experiences and reflection are necessary to good judgment.

But the first step is to engage the text with a reading stance that might be likened to Rosenblatt's "aesthetic" reading—a stance in which the "reader's primary concern is with what happens *during* the actual reading event" (Rosenblatt 24). In these passages, Wordsworth encourages his readers to move away from what Rosenblatt calls "efferent" reading—measuring, analyzing, conceptualizing, and judging—and toward a complete immersion in the *experience* that emerges from their process of reading. Over time, they will become better judges of the experiences offered by the poems, but only if they enter fully into those experiences first.

Rosenblatt's continuum of reading stances, running from efferent to aesthetic, and Berman's distinction between "nonparticipating" to "participating" consciousnesses, can provide a helpful basis for examining the continuum of *perceptual* stances. There can be little doubt that we have many modes of perception, running from "nonparticipating" or "instrumental" or "efferent" at one extreme toward "participating" or "immersive" or "aesthetic" at the other extreme. The "nonparticipating" mode involves objectification and reliance on existing forms and concepts. We see a "tree" while driving by it, but we often do not engage it at all. It is, at that moment, a category rather than an experience. When we climb a tree, on the other hand, we are much more likely to engage it as an experience: to notice its textures and colors and shapes. Berman's argument about modern consciousness might be summarized this way: we have locked ourselves into a speeding car, going somewhere directed by rational purposes, and even though we "see" the world as we speed through it toward our destination, we rarely engage it and participate in it. We assume certain things about experience, and then they become our experience. That's the puzzling thing about perception. We can continually renew it, or we can run it on "automatic."

Wordsworth recognized that perception can be purposive, exclusionary, and bound by "pre-established codes of decision." But he also knew from his own experience that it can sometimes be exciting, renewing, and engaging. As Wordsworth writes in the Prefaces, "the human mind is capable of being excited without the application of gross and violent stimulants" (*1802 Pref, PW* 1: 129). And he set himself the task of generating such excitement in the minds of his readers:

> It has therefore appeared to me, that to endeavour to produce or enlarge this capability is one of the best services in which, at any period, a Writer can be engaged; but this service, excellent at all times, is especially so at the present day. For a multitude of causes, unknown to former times, are now acting with a combined force to blunt the discriminating powers of the mind, and, unfitting it for all voluntary exertion, to reduce it to a state of almost savage torpor. (*1802 Pref, PW* 1: 129).

This passage shows the urgency with which Wordsworth seeks to develop the capability of his readers to be "excited without the application of gross and violent stimulants." And it seems that the excitement of the mind that Wordsworth seeks can only be accomplished by a mode of perception that is paradoxically both *active*—in engaging and participating in experience—and *passive*—in letting go of pre-established categories.

Wordsworth dramatizes this dynamic in the Matthew poems—"Expostulation and Reply" and "The Tables Turned." These two poems provide a nice point of entry for re-reading Wordsworth. The apparent simplicity of the direct confrontations that they represent makes it easy to reduce their meaning to formulaic dualisms between Nature and "book knowledge," between personal pleasure and social purpose, and between "dreaming" and practical doing. Yet the confrontations portrayed, and the positions represented, and the meta-forms used, embody some of the central complexities of Wordsworth's view of language and knowledge and challenge us as readers to re-evaluate our own views.

Poems like these offer a serious and carefully-constructed view of knowledge which is typically distorted by readings that remain entrenched in the model of knowledge that the poems attempt to remake. Our "pre-established codes of decision" place us on the side of Matthew, expecting knowledge to be a matter of acquisition and long study, involving books and intense effort. While we sympathize with William, we cannot take his views very seriously for the same reason that Matthew cannot. We find William appealing, and delightful, but we consider his position to be a pleasant escape rather than a serious view of knowledge. Idle pleasure is no way to learn.

Yet, if we can suspend judgment long enough to consider the ramifications of these poems, we begin to recognize the practicality and power of William's claims. He is the one, he says, that is engaged in serious learning. He is the one who is perceiving, and listening, and conversing with his direct experience.

Apparently we have two poems that disparage book learning and suggest that we are better off just sitting around and communing with "Nature." In "Expostulation and Reply," Matthew argues that William should stop "dream[ing] his time away," and that he should instead edify himself with long and deep study of the wisdom recorded in books. Explicitly, Matthew claims that (1) William will not learn much by sitting out in the woods on an old grey stone and (2) real wisdom has already been established by thinkers who have come before us—we must study them, not "Nature," to become wise ourselves. Implicitly, he also suggests that William is not doing himself or anyone else any real good just sitting there doing *nothing*.

In "The Tables Turned," the persona encourages someone to leave their books and to come outside to experience the beauty of Nature. He asserts that we can learn more "of moral evil and of good" from "One impulse from a vernal wood" than from long-winded written accounts. He claims that books are "a dull and endless strife," and that the reader should "let Nature be your teacher." As opposed to Matthew, who claims that books are "that light bequeath'd / To Beings else forlorn and blind," the persona here argues that we should "Come out into the light of things" where we can experience "spontaneous wisdom" and "truth" directly.

Wordsworth sets up an apparent dichotomy here between "Nature" and "book knowledge," yet he sets it up in a book. Does that lead to inconsistency? On one level, yes. But moving to a higher level, and remembering Wordsworth's insistence that "Poetry is the breath and finer spirit of all knowledge," we can see that Wordsworth is implying something about the use of language here.

In the Advertisement to the 1798 edition of *Lyrical Ballads*, in which these poems first appeared, Wordsworth states that "The lines entitled Expostulation and Reply, and those which follow, arose out of conversation with a friend who was somewhat unreasonably attached to modern books of moral philosophy" (*Adv, PW* 1: 117). This is an important thing to keep in mind, because Wordsworth is implicitly conveying something about writing by making a distinction between "books of moral philosophy" (the language of systems and mental models) and "poetry" (the language of perception and experience).

The Matthew poems embody his attempt to distinguish between "fitting things to words" and "fitting words to things." By writing them and inviting readers to read them, he makes clear his belief that language can be used to engage and extend perception. But the "conversations" dramatized in the poem also undermine the use of language to "pigeonhole" experience—to treat mental models and systems as knowledge which is more valid and significant than personal experience.

Several key concepts appear throughout these poems: death and life, concern with purposive activity, concern with participation in living experience. Matthew's problem with the activity of the persona in

"Expostulation and Reply" is simple: this person is not engaged in any real experience. He is just sitting there, "dreaming" his time away. Time that would be better spent *studying* and *learning* from *books*. Without even knowing it, Matthew points out the shortcoming of his own position when he labels the wisdom of books "the spirit breathed / From dead men to their kind." This is an intriguing construction because it (1) associates book knowledge with death, and (2) suggests that those who live in books are like the dead men who wrote them. Because they too are knowledge seekers? Or because they too are removed from life?

The final stanza can easily be read as a partial acknowledgment of Matthew's criticism, because it returns to "dreaming." But the power of "this mighty sum of things forever speaking" remains. And the stanza is constructed to echo what Matthew said, not to acknowledge it. William asserts that he is "Conversing as I may," engaging the world with his active mind. He injects this claim in the midst of repeating Matthew's initial complaint: "I sit upon this old grey stone / And dream my time away." William counterpoises "Conversing" with "dreaming," suggesting that his behavior is a form of vital interaction rather than self-absorption or idleness.

These poems suggest that perception must be both active (go out and experience, "converse," and so on) and passive ("wise passiveness" and "a heart that listens and receives"). Again, what seems to be a contradiction on one level makes perfect sense at a higher level. The activity demanded of the perceiver is engagement, awareness, and involvement. As most of us know, listening is not a passive process. The "passivity" involves openness to new possibilities, letting go of "pre-established codes of decision" and mental models.

While the poems suggest that immediate experience should be the center of all valuable knowing, they acknowledge the fact that reading, too, can be a form of immediate experience. And while they stress individual perception, they embed it in "Nature." "Nature" in these poems, as in all of Wordsworth's compositions, represents something more than trees and stones. It is a larger mind that co-creates with us. Wordsworth does not allow the dichotomy of Coleridge between the individual mind and a world of "dead matter." Bacon said to "vex Nature"; Wordsworth counters with "witness and learn from Nature." The former is the stance of a human acting on a dead material world to do as he or she pleases, the latter is the stance of a human interacting with a living world—not a world of "gods" in the naive sense, but a world that has its own self-regulating, living state of being.

And the poems also suggest that if we cultivate a "wise passiveness" then we are not always seeking, aiming, limiting our vision and perception by placing it in the framework of "pre-established codes of decision." The "artist's knowledge" that Wordsworth sought to bring back into his culture was the awareness that creativity is always founded in relationships between levels of context—in seeing and embodying the relationship of the "big picture" and the significance of the most minute detail within it. It is only by treating every new experience as an "excursion" into new knowing rather than as an "extension" of pre-existing knowledge or as a perceptual encounter to be viewed *by* pre-existing knowledge, that we can grow and learn without the determinism that his colleagues feared.

Our aims, within our individual contexts, always determine our results. In order to learn, then, we must sometimes be "aimless" or "open." Far from being lazy, such aimlessness is a discipline in and of itself—it is zazen, for the Zen monk; it is the undirected process of beginning to shape a pot as it is thrown, of looking for the form in the matter; it is the recognition that the various compartments of our lives may be connected in significant ways. Such "aimlessness" or "openness" is what enables us to see the "patterns which connect" the field of our aims and the larger field of human and ecological values and needs. It is one highly significant mode of perception that Wordsworth attempted to cultivate in himself and his readers.

Perception was always a function of personal experience, as Wordsworth stated in the "Essay on Morals." And "open" perception was, for him, the prerequisite for meaningful and moral knowledge. But how can such "open" perception be attained? And how can it be directed (or should it be)? What sorts of "functional relationships" can provide coherence in a world of "subjective" perceivers? Aren't Wordsworth's positions, in effect, an acknowledgment of solipsism? Wordsworth struggles with this problem, as critics have noted, but he struggles with it intellectually as well as experientially. His writings indicate that he based his epistemology on some universals that were different from the ones that had been used to ground "objective" science. Rather than accepting a vision of a pre-existing "reality" which was mechanical and which would yield to mental analysis, he offered a vision of Nature as a larger Mind that encompasses and includes the individual perceiver. Rather than stressing accurate concepts and mental models, he stressed the representational nature of all knowing. And rather than founding "relationship" on the products of mind (Truths), he founded it on common processes and structures of mind (which could be tuned to the larger minds of which the individual mind played a part).

The next two chapters argue that Wordsworth struggled to articulate a vision of human mental process which was grounded in perception, yet which recognized that perception itself is a creative event; which stressed the power of habits of mind, yet which recognized that habits of mind could be tuned and improved over time; and which centered on the making and sharing of representations of experience—always artful— rather than the reporting of "truth" and "fact." Wordsworth attempted to develop what might well be called an ecology of mind which stressed connections and relationships, allowing for creativity and identity to emerge from physical experience without being mechanically limited to that experience.[3] He set out to do what Bateson has done more incisively in our own century: to develop a recursive and self-correcting model of mental process, and to extend the category of "mind" outside the individual human head and into the natural and cultural processes in which we are all embedded.

Chapter 6
Wordsworth's Ecology of Mind

> ...they have advised me to prefix a systematic defence of the theory upon which the Poems were written. But I was unwilling to undertake the task, knowing that on this occasion the Reader would look coldly upon my arguments, since I might be suspected of having been principally influenced by the selfish and foolish hope of *reasoning* him into an approbation of these particular Poems: and I was still more unwilling to undertake the task, because, adequately to display the opinions, and fully to enforce the arguments, would require a space wholly disproportionate to a preface. For, to treat the subject with the clearness and coherence of which it is susceptible, it would be necessary to give a full account of the present state of the public taste in this country, and to determine how far this taste is healthy or depraved; which, again, could not be determined, without pointing out in what manner language and the human mind act and re-act on each other, and without tracing the revolutions, not of literature alone, but likewise of society itself.
> —William Wordsworth, 1802 Preface to *Lyrical Ballads*

This epigraph indicates that Wordsworth thought it was possible—though he was not ready to do it—to come to clear and coherent descriptions of the complex interrelationships that make up living systems. Yet as the "Essay on Morals" indicates, he was also suspicious of systematic thinking that imposed itself on those living systems. Systematic thinking as it had been done by eighteenth-century philosophers was missing something vitally important: an awareness of change and recursiveness and complex interrelationships. He did not have the critical tools to describe this problem, but the passage above and the statements he made in the "Essay on Morals" indicate that he sensed it.

Despite our cultural predispositions, more and more thinkers are recognizing that it is possible, as Wordsworth suggested, to be rigorous without being "systematic." Gregory Bateson suggests in his work that to be rigorous in our relationships with others, with nature, and with culture, we must forever refuse to fall into—or at least to finalize—"systematic" constructions which take on a life of their own. All too often, he claims, we mistake the "map" of our conceptions and ideas for the "territory" of experience.[1] In order to overcome that tendency we must find a way to return to perception with an open mind—a task that is very difficult given the limiting nature of systematic thinking and of language itself. In *Wholeness and the Implicate Order*, physicist David Bohm claims that

> clarity of perception and thought evidently requires that we be generally aware of how our experience is shaped by the insight (clear or confused) provided by the theories that are implicit or explicit in our general ways of thinking. To this end, it is useful to emphasize that experience and knowledge are one process, rather than to think that our knowledge is *about* some sort of separate experience. (6)

In one chapter, Bohm attempts—like Wordsworth—to generate a "language of relationship" that can provide a better means for examining thinking and the "content" of thought as aspects of an undivided process. He asserts that what we really need when thinking is "an act of understanding" rather than an "explanation" (56).

But generating a language of relationship requires that we acknowledge and even foster all kinds of complexity. The appeal of logic and systematic thinking comes precisely from their ability to reduce complex relationships to a set of manageable, clear, distinct ideas. For example, in *Polestar of the Ancients* Hayden attempts to make Wordsworth's theory more understandable by claiming that critics have conflated his "literary theory," which remains Aristotelian, with his "creative theory," which is based on eighteenth-century psychological speculations. Hayden's aim—and it is the fundamental aim of analytical thinking—is to find a "fault line" in our thinking about a subject, and to cleave a complex whole into two or more manageable parts. In this case, the "fault line" lies between ideas concerning creative process—poesis—and ideas concerning expression and style. Hayden makes the assumption that the two questions 'What makes a poem beautiful?' and 'Where does a poem come from?' are separate, and separable, questions. And by doing so, he is able to put the answers to each question in separate places and to achieve a sort of clarity.

But the evidence shows that the fault line that Hayden chooses would not have been accepted by Wordsworth, who saw these two questions as only two of many integrated questions to be asked concerning the complex recursive processes of mind. Wordsworth's interest in psychology, and in the dynamics of perception, is the central organizing principle from which all of his compositions emerge. Those compositions are the embodiment of "poetry" as an ongoing activity of mind rather than a product to be "appreciated." Wordsworth was attempting to show that literary theory was only one branch of creative theory—indeed, that science and "knowledge" themselves were branches of creative theory. He refused to accept the idea that "creative theory" could be separated from "objective thinking."

The connection between "creative theory" and "objective thinking" is *representation*. How do we arrive at a picture of the world? By way of *two* languages: the language of biological representation (perception) and the language of symbolic representation (thought). For at least two important reasons, many thinkers have tried to minimize the first and to place the second in control. First, the assumption has been that the senses are less intelligent, less human, than the intellect. To admit that we are "slaves" of sensation seems to place us in the company of animals (is that so bad?). And second, we have less conscious control of perception and sensation. To admit them as shaping factors in our knowing is to admit that reason is not enough to make good judgments in itself.

But Wordsworth sensed, and thinkers like Bateson have begun to make clear, a way to tie "feeling" (sensation/emotion) and "thinking" together into a pattern of knowing that is neither reductive (requiring mind to be limited to physical "associations" of biological input), nor "spiritualized" (requiring that spirit/mind/imagination be separate from, and somehow superadded to, physical processes), nor merely "instrumental" (requiring perception to be a mirror and reason to be the prime operator on perception). The first two formulations are based on the mind-body formulation of Descartes; the third is the uneasy compromise of scientific epistemology, which tends to view reason as the power to do things and self-consciously avoids questions of personal meaning and value.

Relating Perception, "Feeling," and Thinking

One much-misrepresented passage from the Preface provides a good basis for examining Wordsworth's ecology of mind. In this passage,

Wordsworth defines poetry—in terms that have been appropriated by subsequent romantic authors and theorists—as "the spontaneous overflow of powerful feelings." The remainder of this passage, which is extensive, has either been overlooked or assumed to be Wordsworth's attempt to come up with a creative theory based on associationism.[2] Neither approach can acknowledge its full relevance within the broader context of Wordsworth's epistemology. Immediately after defining "all good poetry" as the "spontaneous overflow of powerful feelings," Wordsworth warns his reader that

> though this be true, Poems to which any value can be attached were never produced on any variety of subjects but by a man who, being possessed of more than usual organic sensibility, had also thought long and deeply. For our continued influxes of feeling are modified and directed by our thoughts, which are indeed the representatives of all our past feelings; and, as by contemplating the relations of these general representatives to each other, we discover what is really important to men, so, by the repetition and continuance of this act, our feelings will be connected with important subjects, till at length, if we be originally possessed of much sensibility, such habits of mind will be produced, that, by obeying blindly and mechanically the impulses of those habits, we shall describe objects, and utter sentiments, of such a nature, and in such connection with each other, that the understanding of the Reader must necessarily be in some degree enlightened, and his affections strengthened and purified. (*1802 Pref, PW* 1: 127)

I quote extensively here to provide complete context. In this passage and many others, Wordsworth struggles to articulate his ecological model of mental processes. He connects mind and world, feeling and thinking, conscious and unconscious processes, and the minds of poet and reader in ways that are unprecedented (and seemingly inexplicable) within the dictates of prevailing Cartesian dualisms.

In essence, Wordsworth claims that our "habits" involve our modes of perceiving, of thinking about and representing our experiences, and of considering the relationship between perceptions and conceptions. All of these "habits" involve patterns of *relationship*—between ourselves and the world we perceive, between our senses and our thoughts, and between the relations of senses and thoughts at one point in time to the relation of senses and thoughts at another point in time. The primary reason that Wordsworth cannot subscribe to the systematic thinking of a Godwin or a Paley is the failure of those systems to establish working fields of relationship, working contexts within which to understand and apply the "propositions" that they propound. From the start, he is more concerned with the field of relationships—between mind and world, author and reader, self and other—than with the essence of "things." And he recognizes that all of the relationships he explores are complex, multi-layered, recursive, and potentially self-correcting. He steps outside of constructed dualisms such as mind versus world, body versus mind, and feeling versus thought and replaces them with some principles that are very similar to those of systems thinking and cybernetics. The following discussion offers some of those principles and connects Wordsworth to them.

Emergent Patterns of Organization

One of the fears of Wordsworth's time was that empirical, "associative" views of mental process necessarily led to a biological determinism. This was a major point of dissension between Wordsworth and Coleridge, as embodied in Coleridge's rejection of Wordsworth's views of imagination in the *Biographia Literaria*. Coleridge worked from the conviction that to embed mind in physical processes was to "reduce" it to those processes. He preferred to see imagination as a spiritual principle, a repetition of the divine "I AM." Wordsworth's conviction that imagination evolved from processes of perception made no sense to Coleridge, because it reduced imagination to mere "association" (what he would have called "fancy").

But Coleridge's fear of reductionism originated in a failure to recognize different levels of context, or what Bateson would call different logical types. Cybernetic theorists recognize that the characteristics of a system may not represent the sum of the characteristics of any of the subsystems or entities that make it up. Gradually, environmental scientists and physicists, among others, have grown to understand that what have been called "emergent" systemic behaviors—those that cannot be inferred from the behaviors of the individuals within the system or from the original conditions of the system—are not only possible, but expected. For example, it is possible to predict when and how a liquid will begin to boil, but there is no way to infer that information from the behavior of an individual molecule that will start the process. It is also possible to recognize that water consists of a relationship between Hydrogen and Oxygen atoms, but one cannot infer the behavior of water from the behavior of those atoms before they enter the system "water."³ And these are inorganic systems. Emergence is even more significant in organic, living systems. In effect, whole living systems are always greater than the sum of the parts that constitute them.⁴ Thus it is possible to accept a view of knowing which emerges from physical processes, yet which is not limited to a reductive "behaviorism" like that of B. F. Skinner.

Wordsworth shows his awareness of a principle of emergence in many of his compositions. In an illuminating passage which appears in identical form in the *Two-Part Prelude* and the *1805 Prelude*, he states outright that (1) there are biological origins for our intellectual life and (2) we cannot trace each of our thoughts back to its biological origins in physical sensation and experience. In the process of discussing the growth of his mind, he steps back a moment and writes:

> But who shall parcel out
> His intellect by geometric rules
> Split like a province into round and square?
> Who knows the individual hour in which
> His habits were first sown even as a seed?
> Who that shall point as with a wand, and say
> 'This portion of the river of my mind
> Came from yon fountain'?
> ...
> And thou wilt doubt with me, less aptly skilled
> Than many are to class the cabinet
> Of their sensations, and in voluble phrase
> Run through the history and birth of each
> As of a single independent thing.
> Hard task to analyse a soul, in which
> Not only general habits and desires,
> But each most obvious and particular thought—
> Not in a mystical and idle sense,
> But in the words of reason deeply weighed—
> Hath no beginning. (2: 242–67)

Important in these passages are the non-dualistic connections implied structurally between "sensations" and "soul" ("mind" in the 1850 *Prelude*) and between "habits," "desires," and "thought." Our habits and desires and thoughts all emerge from processes that connect our unconscious and conscious minds, our physical and mental states of being, according to Wordsworth. He insists that to recognize and accept this fact is rational and vital to understanding the limits of human knowing. He does not seek a mystical position, but a starting point for an understanding of mental process that allows for thoughts and identities—"minds"—to emerge from the biological foundations of perception and experience.

Pleroma and Creatura: The *Difference* of Living Systems

Bateson provides a nice way to conceptualize the workings of mental process as emergent from, and yet not completely determined by, physical processes. The complexity of representation and reaction to representation is one of the amazing qualities of mind. The element that makes such emergence of higher-level patterns possible is, according to Bateson, the ability to recognize and respond to *difference*. In essence, Bateson attempts to solve the mind/matter problem NOT by unifying the two categories or by subordinating one to the other (mind is simply the result of certain material manifestations—or matter is simply a by-product of mind), but by offering a different, and potentially more useful, dichotomy.

In *Mind and Nature*, he builds his ideas on Jung's distinction between the "pleroma," or nonliving things, and the "creatura," or living things. He asserts that the laws of physical science are adequate for dealing with the pleroma. Linear cause-effect modeling is adequate to the task of analyzing the behavior of billiard balls when struck. But the creatura are different because of the fact that they recognize and act on the basis of *difference itself*. In other words, no energy need be input to make an animal respond to a new situation. The stimuli that thinking entities respond to are stimuli consisting of differences, not simply stimuli consisting of physical force or energy. And this means that neither the physical modeling of the laws of thermodynamics nor the abstract modeling of linear logic can accommodate the complexities of thinking response. Bateson asserts the importance of preserving in our theories the "biological nature (cybernetic, hierarchic, holistic, non-linear, systemic nature—call it what you will) of the world and our relations to it" (*Angels Fear* 99). He insists that we must develop a "Creatural science" that accounts for mental process:

> Let us not pretend that mental phenomena can be mapped onto the behavior of billiard balls. (*Angels Fear* 99)

This position should sound familiar, because it is precisely the position that Wordsworth felt compelled to take in the late eighteenth century. He did not have the critical vocabulary that Bateson has been able to call on, but he had a very clear sense that understanding "mental phenomena" was absolutely vital to the future of human knowing. Indeed, he says in the 1800 Preface that the perception of "similitude in dissimilitude"

> is the great spring of the activity of our minds, and their chief feeder. From this principle the direction of the sexual appetite, and all the passions connected with it, take their origin: it is the life of our ordinary conversation; and upon the accuracy with which similitude in dissimilitude, and dissimilitude in similitude are perceived, depend our taste and our moral feelings. (*1802 Pref, PW* 1: 149)

Here Wordsworth asserts that the issue of *difference* (which Bateson cites as the key to mindful behavior) is central to the biological, social, and moral functioning of living beings. He asserts that everything is connected, and that being able to recognize difference and likeness and the relations between the two is essential to meaningful life. And difference is, by its nature, a matter of relationship and representation, rather than a matter of "thingness."

Levels of Mental Process: We are Parts of Larger Minds

In *Mind and Nature*, Bateson outlines the characteristics of mind in such a way as to illustrate that it is possible, indeed desirable, to see as "mindful" many "systems" that we would not traditionally regard as such. Like an ant colony, which behaves as if it were a single mind and yet contains ants which act according to their own rudimentary minds, systems such as human families, cultures, and ecosystems may be, in fact, minds which are both constituted by and constitutive of the individual minds at work within them. Mind, for Bateson, is

> a something that can receive information [of difference] and can, through the self-regulation or self-correction made possible by circular trains of causation, maintain the truth of certain propositions about itself. (*Angels Fear* 19)

While this may or may not entail what we consider to be "consciousness" (or, at a higher level of abstraction, "self-consciousness"), it provides a model of mental process in which the activities at one level are informed by and inform the emergent qualities of the next higher level. While an ant may have no conception of the system of which it is a part, it nevertheless exists both as an independent creature that responds to difference and as a player in the patterns of the larger mind. As Bateson says, at every level

> a given mind is likely to be a component or subsystem in some larger and more complex mind, as an individual cell may be a component in an organism, or a person may be a component in a community. The world of mental process opens up into a self-organizing world of Chinese boxes, in which information generates more information. (19)

The boundaries of mind are complicated by Bateson's construction in a way that suits Wordsworth's views well. What has been viewed as his "pantheism" can also be viewed as the awareness of mindful patterns in the natural world—regularities and significant differences that indicate the workings of a larger mind. For example, in the fragment "The Pedlar," later incorporated into *The Excursion*, Wordsworth uses description that explicitly frames the natural world in mental terms:

> —in the after day
> Of boyhood, many an hour in caves forlorn
> And in the hollow depths of naked crags
> He sate, and even in their fixed lineaments,
> Or from the power of a peculiar eye,
> Or by creative feeling overborne,
> Or by predominance of thought oppressed,
> Even in their fixed and steady lineaments
> He traced an ebbing and a flowing mind,
> Expression ever varying. (*Pedlar* 21)

While Wordsworth is careful to equivocate about the source of the Pedlar's insight, the insight remains. One can read this as a mere "subjective projection" resulting from "the power of a peculiar eye" or mental strain, but in the full context of this fragment and of Wordsworth's work as a whole, such a reading is false.

The entire fragment is preoccupied with the varying and problematic connection between this larger mind and the mind of the Pedlar, and it asserts a complementary relationship between the two. The larger mind is unknown to the Pedlar, and yet it shapes and provides the Pedlar with the ground of his being. He experiences moments in which he becomes part of the larger mind, and on reflection he finds conviction and moral knowledge in his awareness of its existence. For example, at one moment,

> Sensation, soul, and form,
> All melted into him; they swallowed up
> His animal being. In them did he live,
> And by them did he live—they were his life.
> In such access of mind, in such high hour
> Of visitation from the living God,
> He did not feel the God, he felt his works.
> Thought was not; in enjoyment it expired.
> Such hour by prayer or praise was unprofaned;
> He neither prayed, nor offered thanks or praise;
> His mind was a thanksgiving to the power
> That made him. It was blessedness and love. (*Pedlar* 23)

The language here is complex, and refuses to yield to dualistic analysis. "Sensation, soul, and form" are three different categories—perception, spirit, and pattern—which are all linked here. They "melted into him" (external moving to internal) *and* "swallowed up / His animal being" (internal moving to external). He lives in them, by them, and is them. The critical phrase here, though, is not "state of mind," but "access of mind." The larger mind and himself become one, and "God" is a familiar placeholder which he posits and then quickly frees of its conceptual freight. He does not pray, he does not reflect, he simply enters the larger mind for a moment: "His mind was a thanksgiving to the power / That made him."

And the final passage of "The Pedlar," which was incorporated into Wordsworth's "epistemic alteration" in Book Three of the 1805 and 1850 *Preludes*, shows all the complexity and beauty of Wordsworth's attempt to conceive of matter in terms of mind and mind in terms of matter:

> From deep analogies by thought supplied,
> Or consciousnesses not to be subdued,
> To every natural form, rock, fruit, and flower,
> Even the loose stones that cover the highway,

> He gave a moral life; he saw them feel,
> Or linked them to some feeling. In all shapes
> He found a secret and mysterious soul,
> A fragrance and a spirit of strange meaning.
> He made it—for it only lived to him,
> And to the God who looked into his mind.
> Such sympathies would often bear him far
> In outward gesture, and in visible look,
> Beyond the common seeming of mankind.
> Some called it madness; such it might have been,
> But that he had an eye which evermore
> Looked deep into the shades of difference
> As they lie hid in exterior forms,
> Near or remote, minute or vast—an eye
> Which from a stone, a tree, a withered leaf,
> To the broad ocean and the azure heavens
> Spangled with kindred multitudes of stars,
> Could find no surface where its power might sleep—
> Which spake perpetual logic to his soul,
> And by an unrelenting agency
> Did bind his feelings even as in a chain. (*Pedlar* 32)

This passage, quoted earlier, connects the mind of the Pedlar to the entire creation in mindlike terms, returning to the perception of difference and similitude (analogies) as the power that finds/makes meaning. The natural world is a field of meaningfulness to the Pedlar, and he recognizes—no, *sees*—that he is part of that field. He had received, in essence, a perceptual education from Nature's hands. And he—and Wordsworth—saw themselves as part of the field of perception, as maker/sharers of meaning within that field.

Systemic and Systematic Modes of Knowing: Calibration and Feedback

An instructive way to look at the difference between philosophical and rhetorical assumptions about knowing is provided by Gregory Bateson in *Angels Fear*. He makes an illuminating distinction, based on Horst Mittelstaedt's work, between two methods of adaptive learning—"feedback" and "calibration." For his example, Bateson compares the actions of a rifleman and a hunter with a shotgun. The rifleman aims, corrects errors, then fires. The shotgun hunter shoots, shoots again, and corrects errors by iteration. The former uses analysis (examination of data in one instance) and relies on conscious methods; the latter uses synthesis (absorption of data from many instances) and relies on long practice. One relies on "propositional" knowledge of a sort, the other on "pragmatic" knowledge.

The rifleman's mode of error correction (or learning) stresses conscious technique and precision and mastery of principles of aiming. Context is not a very significant issue, because the target must be sitting still, in the clear, or moving slowly enough to track, before error-correction can even begin. And if the bird does not fall, then the rifleman's skill is shown to be inadequate. He has failed.

On the other hand, the shotgun shooter's mode of error-correction (or learning) presupposes the importance of experience and practice over many attempts. Context is always an important issue, because the birds will be in chaotic flight when they are "started," and the shooter must judge trajectory and timing on the spot. He or she cannot take time to aim before firing. The pattern of the birds' flights becomes a context for the current action and an education for future actions. The rifleman learns a technique for centering the gun sight; the shotgun shooter learns a pattern of interaction with his prey. To attempt to make conscious corrections during the act of shooting dooms the shotgun hunter to failure. Her success lies in the successful "tuning" of her responses to a variety of particular contexts over time. Whether one bird drops or not has little to do with her ability. When a high percentage of birds drop over time, she shows that she is learning. For the rifleman, every bird that does not drop is a failure of technique.

In fact, actions generally involve both types of error correction to some degree. Learning often appears to be the discussion of feedback and technique when in fact it is a process of calibration. Calibration is learning by "trial and error"; the main thrust of philosophy and science is to remove the necessity for such learning. If our knowledge is general enough, we should be able to act on the basis of principles that are clearly-defined, using techniques that are foolproof, producing results that are inevitable. But on closer inspection, much of life remains a trial and error affair. Any great basketball player will admit that every game is different and that there's no way to explain the results of calibration in terms that do not take context into account. Any parent of a young child will tell you that no matter how many books he or she reads, the decisions about discipline and nurturing and loving that child are made more by trial and error, by calibration over time, than by a "calculus of ends and means." It is interesting that Sebberson calls "sophism" such a calculus, when in fact Platonic philosophy and science are much more prone to such a critique.

Plato placed the category of "Truth" first, and the category of "Good" (ideal order and harmony) became a necessary result of "Truth." In other words, the ideal GOOD state will be set in place by conscious correction of all the errors of the corrupt state. Once we all kneel at the altar of Truth, the Good will inevitably appear. On the other hand, Isocrates put the category of the Good (well-considered speaking and acting leading to positive results) first, and claimed that Truth (firm and unchanging principles which could be taught and used regardless of context) was an occasional and unreliable guide for action.

In this, he followed "sophists" or "rhetoricians" such as Gorgias and Protagoras who stressed the importance of *kairos*— the context in which moral decisions about what to say and do were made. One cannot teach virtue, then, but one can teach modes of relationship that encourage virtuous decision-making and action within each context dealt with. Quintilian, a Roman rhetorician whom Wordsworth certainly knew well, took the Isocratean position as well. He went so far as to say that in the pursuit of the Good, the orator might have to bend or misrepresent or disregard the (concept of the) True.

Within an ecology of mind, calibration can only take place by entering into larger mindful processes. The shotgun shooter, for example, must not rely on conscious error correction, but must participate fully in the flow of events—the movement of the birds, the raising of the gun, and the firing—to be successful at "bagging his prey." The basketball player must become one with his team, moving to the right place at the right time, aware of the movements on the court, to play his or her part effectively.

Wordsworth's epistemology depends more on ongoing processes of calibration—entering larger mindlike processes, tuning perception, developing good habits of mind, and revising mental models over time—than on feedback or testing against some pre-established set of aims or ideas. And his awareness of classical rhetoric provided him with a conceptual framework for incorporating processes of calibration into his model of knowing.

Chapter 7
Representation and Rhetoric

This chapter examines Wordsworth's construction of a rhetorical model of knowing—a model that seems similar in some important ways to those of "cybernetics" theorists like Bateson. To do so, it draws on previously undiscussed connections between Quintilian and Wordsworth and returns to some of the "systemic" concepts of Bateson and Antonio Damasio. These thinkers help us to develop an idiom—a language of relationships and interrelationship—that links body and mind, art and science, and mind and nature in the ways that Wordsworth set out to link them in the Prefaces to *Lyrical Ballads*.

The linkages, interestingly enough, return us to the knowledge battle that was waged in ancient Greece between Plato and those he called the Sophists. One of the central points of difference between Plato and the Sophists was a disagreement about the idea of Truth. For Plato, Truth was pre-existing and reachable only by purging oneself of the sensual clutter that interfered with "seeing" it. Truth and knowledge preceded representation in language; thus rhetoric and poetry could both be subordinated to philosophy. When language was used with dialectical method it could lead to truth and knowledge. When used with appropriate rhetorical methods it could transmit truth and knowledge in dilute form to others. But "truth" was to be "found" and not "composed," so language and representation were secondary issues rather than primary issues.

The Sophists, and Isocrates, took a different view. Truth for them was always embedded in context, in the *kairos* or situation at hand. Although they would not have taken the relativist stance of some postmodern critics, they believed that language and representation were the primary issues in knowing. They would not suppose that we could somehow get beyond the realm of *doxa* and into a realm of ideal forms and truth that preceded representation. Protagoras' statement that "man is the measure of all things" can be seen as an indication that our mental representations of experience are what give it value and meaning to us, and therefore all we know exists in the field of human representation and interpretation. Anything that exists outside that field, or that we dismiss from that field, has no essential value for us.

The term *logos* is at the center of this argument. In different contexts it could be taken to mean "reason" or "language" or "argument" or even "reality." Do meaning and truth exist prior to language? Or are they necessarily constructed in language and other systems of symbolic representation? The tradition of philosophy claims the former, and minimizes language's role until the work of Locke and Hume reopened the problems of language and perception as representation. The tradition of rhetoric claims the latter, and claims that language is always central to knowing and constructing meaning. My claim is that Wordsworth drew upon, and extended, the tradition of rhetoric. He would have been reluctant to state this allegiance outright, given the eighteenth-century treatment of rhetoric as the use of language to mislead by moving the emotions rather than reasoning. But Wordsworth's claims about knowing, about language, and about his poetic purposes, fit well with the broader tradition of rhetoric and the more comprehensive views of rhetoric being (re)constructed today by thinkers like Kenneth Burke. In a very real sense, he claimed that the function of poetry was what had been earlier claimed by rhetoric. Since expository writing and science refused rhetoric and treated logos and reality as if they were identical, Wordsworth could not write in that tradition. He claims in the Preface that the primary distinction is not between poetry and prose, but "between poetry and science, or matter of fact." And he defines poetry in rhetorical terms as the construction and sharing of symbolic meaning.

This chapter opens with a discussion of what rhetoric seemed to be in Wordsworth's time and how we are reconstructing the use of the term today. Then it returns to a classical rhetorical source that Wordsworth probably drew on in his effort to develop a representation-centered model of knowing and composing: Quintilian's *Institutes of Oratory*. Quintilian's views of composition and effective communication reveal principles similar to the four that Wordsworth outlined in his "Essay on Morals." They stress the personal origins of knowledge without denying the need for broader consensus, and they build that consensus on shared structures of meditation, mental process, and representation. Although this chapter focuses on Wordsworth's connection to Quintilian, it includes "excursions" that offer additional context and breadth to the developing discussion.

Wordsworth's Relations with Enlightenment "Rhetoric"

Wordsworth began writing in a world in which rhetoric was seen as a tool of false influence and obfuscation. It interfered with clarity and thus was antithetical to enlightenment. Writing that purported to be scientific, or objective, or intellectual, had to be free of the trappings of rhetorical ploys and devices. Philosophy and science were the highest forms of discourse; rhetoric was reserved for poetry and sermons. What happened, of course, was that poets claimed rhetorical figures for themselves and elevated their use to "high art," while writers of serious tracts attempted to do away with "figures" altogether, seeking a transparent and luminous object-oriented language. Wordsworth's complaints about "poetic diction" are rooted in this shift. He sensed that separating the "figures" of speech from the powerful experience that generated them, and separating language itself from the spoken discourse of everyday life, removed rhetoric from the field of meaning-making where it belonged and placed it in the service of abstract philosophy and science.[1]

In outline, the enlightenment position on rhetoric can be summarized by Alexander Pope's famous couplet:

> True wit is Nature to advantage dressed,
> What oft was thought, but ne'er so well expressed.

Pope, like Wordsworth, claims "Nature" as a baseline for meaning in discourse. But then he asserts that Nature is, in essence, equivalent to "What oft was thought"—a construction that implies two important things:

1. "Nature" is the same thing as "what we know and have articulated about Nature," and
2. Thought and expression are fundamentally separated. Ideas are conceived, and then we use language to express those ideas to others.

This position on rhetoric is firmly rooted in Plato's *Phaedrus*, where Socrates claims that good rhetoric is always secondary to good philosophy. One knows, then one phrases that knowing in ways that allow its transmission—either between "philosopher-kings" or between "philosopher-kings" and "lesser souls."

Newtonian science had helped to buttress this Platonic position in many ways. A real, objective world preceded all representation, which then had to be measured for "truth" or "accuracy" against that real, objective world. Valuable efforts to know aimed to represent more accurately the structure of things that pre-existed all knowing. Rhetoric played no role in this process, because it involved feelings and opinions and all the confusing complexities of human life. To bring rhetoric into science would undermine the validity of scientific knowledge, and threaten a return to the Dark Ages.

Our critical construction of eighteenth-century poetry as "Public" and rhetorically-engaged, and of nineteenth-century poetry as typified by a retreat into "Private" and anti-rhetorical stances, is based on curious definitions of the terms "rhetoric," "Public," and "Private." Although the poetry of Pope is considered to be "rhetorical" and "didactic," it is obvious that Newton's metaphorical construction ("world-as-machine") had much more rhetorical force than any of Pope's poems. And while Wordsworth has been deemed "expressive" and "solitary," his poems are much more likely to *move* a reader than the highly-stylized, intellect-centered poems of Swift, Pope, and Dryden. Eighteenth-century poetry tended to be heavy on the use of rhetorical figures and tropes, but it used them as a glaze over the existing politicosocial and scientific models—a sort of candy coating for the pill of pre-existing, and apparently necessary, constructions of knowledge (power). And with the limited audience that these authors had, can we call their work "Public"? Is it "public" to write position papers to people who already hold the same positions? To write delightful and glamorous poems and essays which merely reaffirm others in their beliefs?[2]

Wordsworth's poetic stance has been treated as a turning away from the "public" and "rhetorical" character of eighteenth-century poetry, but in actuality it was an effort

1. to make poetry *more* public, more available for engagement by a broader and more multivalent "audience," and
2. to rescue the central tasks of rhetoric (representation, meaning-making, power to move) from both scientific discourse and "poetic diction."

Eighteenth-century science confidently claimed to represent reality. Eighteenth-century poetry, on the other hand, claimed to "represent beautifully." The discourse of science had appropriated "truth" as its domain, and left "beauty," "wit," and "elegance" to the poets. The result was a divorce of "knowledge" from beauty and pleasure, and of objective, material things from subjective, personal experiences and feelings.

Wordsworth's work attempted to forge new links between world and mind, truth and beauty, art and life. And though he would never have applied the term "rhetoric" to what he was doing, Wordsworth was preoccupied with creating a new epistemological stance that recognized and employed the complexities of logos and kairos, of the ongoing dialectic between symbolically-constructed "reality" and the particular situations in which meaning is made and action is taken.

A Broader View of Rhetoric

> As a field for the discussion of belief and the basis of philosophy, rhetoric is concerned with the interface or meeting-place between human beings and the external world. It is concerned with all that people are conscious of and feel that they can approach and understand; and, so, also with all that they feel irreducibly different, unknowable, and beyond understanding. (Hunter 5)

Rhetoric is not simply a matter of how we express our ideas. It forms the field for symbolic constructions of meaning and informs individual acts of symbolic construction. In fact, I will make a radical claim for rhetoric—a claim that makes perfect sense intellectually, yet makes people very uncomfortable because it seems to open up all sorts of philosophical problems. In fact, it seems to annihilate philosophy completely. As a result, it does not garner people's assent very easily or fully. That claim, stated simply, is:

> Rhetoric precedes and circumscribes all philosophy.

A philosophy is a system made up of symbolic representations. Representation is the domain of rhetoric, broadly construed. Before a philosophy can be articulated, the system of representation that it employs and is limited by must be in place—language, logic, and *a priori* assumptions. The development of that system, both in the individual articulating a philosophy and in the readers who are invited to share that philosophy, is a rhetorical venture. It is always an experimental establishment of a boundary system that then seeks assent and furthers its own articulation.

William Wordsworth should not be judged as a philosophical poet, in the traditional sense of "philosophy," but as a rhetorical poet, in the all-encompassing sense of rhetoric offered above. In order to participate in his work effectively, we must recover the complex fullness of the meaning of "rhetoric" from the attacks of philosophers over the centuries—attacks that have attempted to reduce rhetoric to the "style" and "delivery" of preconceived "subject matter" (Platonic view) or that treat rhetoric as a "subject matter" without connecting it to the world of "Nature" (poststructuralist view—de Man, Kneale, and so on). Both these views place rhetoric in a subordinate position and treat it as a matter of style and delivery. For Plato, rhetoric is always subordinated to, and should be controlled by, logos (reality). For some poststructural thinkers, rhetoric is a matter of figures, but figures are all we have. There is no "reality" that exists prior to or outside of the logos (symbolic construction of reality). But if rhetoric is seen as a boundary-defining process, as the place at which the unknown and the symbolically-constructed meet, then it becomes highly significant.

Following the work of Kenneth Burke, I assert that rhetoric is the use of symbolic action to effect changes in the structuring of experience into "reality." I would like to oppose rhetoric to deconstruction, rather than allowing deconstructionists to appropriate rhetoric as their own domain in the "world-as-text." From the Sophists of ancient Greece (and Isocrates) we have a tradition in rhetoric which has often been ignored completely: a tradition which makes rhetoric a reconstructive rather than a deconstructive activity. The purpose of rhetoric, within this tradition, is to establish new "positions of authority" within the kairos, or situation-at-hand. Such new positions of authority require that some voices be subordinated to others, that some positions be abandoned while others are held. They operate not in the realm of "absolute truths," but functional judgments. And they never lose touch with perception itself. In short, they offer a flexible and incremental approach to evaluating and changing modes of relationship, rather than a set of either/or dichotomies and unattainable absolutes.

The Classical Connection: Quintilian's *Institutes of Oratory*

Wordsworth's convictions that "images" and "impressions" move us more than "bald & naked reasonings," that we most often base our decisions on habits of mind rather than on abstract reasoning, and that language should attempt to take the shape of experience rather than corralling it, have firm foundations in rhetorical theory all the way back to the Sophists of ancient Greece. Indeed, to understand Wordsworth's representation-centered model of knowing and discourse, we must recontextualize his ideas about composition within the tradition of classical rhetoric.[3]

Wordsworth's connections with classical writers have been largely unexplored because of critical preconceptions about both the "classical tradition" and Wordsworth's poetic theories and practices. Generally the two just don't seem to match closely enough in outline to deserve careful comparison. The "classical tradition," especially the Latin tradition to which Wordsworth would have had the greatest exposure, was the guiding light of the eighteenth century. It stressed decorum, balance, and restraint; it extolled the virtues of public service and civic duty; it concerned itself with the beauty of created things, with the balance and proportion and elegance achieved by art. Wordsworth, on the other hand, opened his poetic career with statements that stressed feeling and passion. He seemed more interested in experiencing the process by which things are created than in cataloging the properties of the things themselves. His work centered on personal expression, despite claims of public purpose, and he stressed nature and sincerity of expression over art and elegance. These were some of the differences that set Wordsworth apart from his eighteenth-century predecessors and, as a result, seemed to place him outside the classical tradition.

One of the obvious but little-observed problems with this familiar formula is its reduction of a multiplicity of classical voices to a monolithic "tradition." The neoclassicism of the eighteenth century relied heavily on selected ideas of selected classical thinkers. It did not by any means appropriate a complete "classical tradition." While this point seems simplistic, it is all too often overlooked in our desire to place ideas into clear categories.

If the idea of a monolithic "classical tradition" is put aside, the very elements of Wordsworth's thinking which seem to separate him from that tradition lead us to fascinating connections with a classical figure of great importance—Quintilian. Wordsworth says little of Quintilian in his letters and other prose writings, but it is certain that he knew the Institutes well.[4] Worthington reminds us that Wordsworth owned two copies of Quintilian's *Institutes of Oratory* in the original Latin—versions edited by R. Whitaker (1641) and H. Cruttendon (1695) (Worthington 77). She also asserts that Wordsworth was conversant with Latin, supporting her claim by citing Wordsworth's extensive use of Latin quotations in his letters and De Quincey's firsthand statement that Wordsworth "'...by reading the lyric poetry of Horace, simply for his own delight as a student of composition, made himself a master of Latinity in its most difficult form'" (Worthington 16). Her interest, however, lies in Wordsworth's use of Latin historical writings; she says nothing in her text about his appropriations and literary uses of classical rhetoric.

John Nabholtz pursues Wordsworth's interest in and use of classical rhetoric a bit further. He asserts the inevitable influence of classical rhetorical tradition, "in which all the Romantics had been trained since their grammar school days" ("Classical Rhetoric" 119), on romantic prose writings, and suggests that failure to recognize this influence is a significant critical omission. He asserts that the romantic poets, along with all students of that day and age,

> probably first encountered the name of Quintilian in Jean Heuzet's *Selectae e Profanis Scriptoribus Historiae*, an anthology of very short selections from the Roman writers used in the third or fourth year of school for translation exercises and as a source of topics for English and Latin themes. (119)

Nabholtz cites further evidence of exposure to Quintilian; "later in his grammar-school training" the student

> would have encountered Scriptores Romani, a popular Eton anthology with extended selections from Quintilian and from Cicero's *Orator*, *De Inventione*, *De Oratore*, and *De Claribus Oratoribus*, among other texts. (119)

Indeed, Nabholtz writes, "Byron spoke for most of his contemporaries when in 1807 he included Demosthenes, Cicero, and Quintilian among those authors we [sic] knew so well that he could 'quote passages from any mentioned'" (120). Nabholtz makes a strong case for the further exploration of romantic uses of classical rhetoric. Much of his argument, however, is devoted to Coleridge's prose writings; he makes no claims about Wordsworth and does not offer a close examination of Quintilian's rhetorical ideas.5

With the work of Worthington and Nabholtz in mind, a closer examination of Wordsworth's use of classical sources seems in order. Wordsworth signals his interest in Quintilian's ideas by quoting from the *Institutes of Oratory* in a letter to Charles James Fox dated January 14, 1801 in which he explains his poetic purposes. Fox was one of the "persons of eminence either in Letters or in the state" (*LWDW* 310) selected to receive a complimentary copy of the *Lyrical Ballads*; this letter was sent along with the volumes in the hopes of enhancing the book's reputation and potential for success despite the fact that it was "written upon a theory professedly new, and on principles which many persons will be unwilling to admit" (*LWDW* 310). Wordsworth's discussions in this letter of his poetic purposes and his social aims are earnest and impassioned, and the use of the Institutes here suggests that Wordsworth might have found Quintilian a classical authority whose ideas lent weight to his "professedly new" theories.

Like Wordsworth, and unlike many of his contemporaries, Quintilian offered a moral vision that centered on excellence of personal expression, which stressed feeling (and, implicitly, sensation) as a more powerful and universal principle than reason, and which placed art secondary to "nature." Quintilian's *Institutes of Oratory* outlines rhetorical principles and theories of composition that resonate strongly with the conceptions of poetic purpose and creative theory put forth by Wordsworth in his early letters and in the Preface to *Lyrical Ballads*. Quintilian dedicates an entire book to the formation of "habits of mind" by way of reading, meditation, and composition—a focus on creative theory that Kennedy claims is unique in rhetorical treatises of the classical period. He insists that feeling, rather than rational argument, is the "life and soul of eloquence," and that it should be the primary interest of the orator; yet he insists that feeling and thought are always interconnected, that powerful spontaneous expression arises only from experience and reflection. He claims that the only way to move others is to be moved ourselves, that sincerity of feeling and facility of imagination lead to moving expression. In short, he develops a rhetorical theory that is intensely private, starting with the formation of the individual's mind and his ability to feel and leading to authentic personal expression which moves others because it is authentic.

The quote from Quintilian that Wordsworth cites in his letter to Charles James Fox occurs in a passage that stresses the importance of two poems—"Michael" and "The Brothers"—as indicators of Wordsworth's poetic purposes and aims. "The two poems which I have mentioned," Wordsworth writes,

> were written with a view to shew that men who do not wear fine cloaths can feel deeply. "Pectus enim est quod disertos facit et vis mentis. Ideoque imperitus quoque, si modo sint aliquo affectu concitati, verba non desunt." The poems are faithful copies from nature; and I hope, whatever effect they have upon you, you will at least be able to perceive that they may excite profitable sympathies in many kind and good hearts, and may in some small degree enlarge our feelings of reverence for our species, and our knowledge of human nature ... (*LWDW* 315)

Wordsworth concludes the letter by expressing his hope that the poems will "co-operate, however feebly, with the illustrious efforts" (*LWDW* 315) Fox has made to remedy social ills.

The Latin quote in this passage, de Selincourt notes, comes from "Quintilian, Inst. Orat. x. vii. 15" (*LWDW* 315). Watson's translation of this passage reads

> for it is strength of feeling combined with energy of intellect that renders us eloquent. Hence even to the illiterate words are not wanting, if they be but roused by some strong passion. (Quintilian 2: 304)

Several familiar elements are at play here—a stress on "feeling" and "passion"; democratic leanings; a desire to speak in the "language of real men." What Quintilian advocates in the *Institutes*, and what Wordsworth responds to in Quintilian, is a representation-based view of knowing which begins with personal perceptual representations of experience and expands into shared representations of the good and the true in the public domain. Quintilian offers a model not only of "effective communication," but of composition-centered knowing and meaning-making.

Excursion: Reason and Habits of Mind

Wordsworth's development of the idea of "habits of mind" is consistent with his pervasive concern about "pre-established codes of decision." He never sought to overthrow Second Nature because that would result in a disaster like the French Revolution. The French Revolution, and Wordsworth's reaction to it, is indicative of his developing stance concerning habits of mind. In his early phase, he found Godwin's appeal to human reason and revolution in the name of a "better system" to be convincing. He too wanted a "better system" than the one offered by the emerging industrial/scientific culture. But his experiences in France showed him the devastation that follows when attempts are made to overthrow existing forms of Second Nature by means of abstract "systems." Social structures can only bear incremental changes accomplished by recursive processes of reconstructive thinking. Both the individual and culture at large are guided by habits of mind—"clothing" which must not be stripped, but which must be changed carefully over time.

In this view habits of mind, rather than reason, become the central ordering faculty of knowing and acting. And that makes perfect sense within the Wordsworthian canon. In *The Prelude*, he cites the "unreasoning progress of the world," and in the Preface to *Lyrical Ballads* he claims that he has purposes which were not clearly formulated beforehand, but which emerged from his "habits." He tries in the "Essay on Morals" to show that much of what we consider to be reasoning is really rationalization. Arguments are generally constructed to make sense of pre-existing patterns of action; rarely do they provide the basis for those actions. Again, the affective/intuitive field of relationships predominates in Wordsworth's vision. For example, he writes:

> We do not argue in defense of our good actions; we feel internally their beneficent effect. (*EoM, PW* 1: 104)

When we do something that is "unworthy," we look to systems of morality for arguments by which to defend ourselves and to justify our errant actions (and have little trouble finding such systems).

Wordsworth knows that rationalization does not change habits of mind at all—it simply provides a means for reinforcing them. This is the greatest shortcoming of reason divorced from moral judgment—of the division between intellectual clarity and moral judgment typical from Descartes' time forward. Reason cannot be an acceptable guide for action in most cases, because in most cases we must act on the spur of the moment on the basis of preformed habits.

Once the ideal of "objective reason" is removed or subjugated, and Imagination and habits of mind are stressed as central in the making of good judgment and good action, the issues of creativity and psychology and rhetorical effectiveness become interconnected in interesting and somewhat confusing ways. The person hoping to influence another's habits of mind must first "picture" things in such a way that they are "moving" in and of themselves. The goal is not to devise an argument, but an illustration. Of course, this is a well-known strategy (the parables of Christ, for example). By intercourse with and engagement with Nature, the poet develops good habits of mind. And then his work is informed with an evolving purpose that does not have to be explained or argued.

Good habit formation, according to Wordsworth, could be ensured by *experiencing* fully—attending to the "language of the sense" with a "wise passiveness"—and *reflecting* on experience—remediating our "pre-established codes of decision" in the light of new experience. The goal of learning, and the essence of knowledge, then becomes revision, rather than conceptual closure. We should not aim to master "codes of decision," but to develop a stance from which we can remake them continually in the light of our experiential context.

No one can argue an individual into such a position, and no one can simply recreate culture in this image. Wordsworth cannot resort to argument or systematic thinking because both are completely bound by Second Nature. He says

> Now I know no book or system of moral philosophy written with sufficient power to melt into our affections, to incorporate itself with the blood and vital juices of our minds, and thence to have any influence worth our notice in forming those habits of which I am speaking. Perhaps by the plan which these authors pursue this effect is rendered unattainable. (*EoM, PW* 1: 103)

He is seeking an immediacy of effect that can only be equated to direct and moving experience: not cogitation, but gut-felt experience. And that is what the poetry of participation is all about. Only the *power* of particular experiences and mental images associated with them can incrementally change habits of mind. Wordsworth thus seeks an immediacy of description and image, an immediacy that *depends* on the strong and effective use of language (rather than attempting to remove language from the field of play). In short, he seeks to redefine knowing in terms of a *logos*—a symbolically-constructed reality—that both emerges from and shapes every *kairos* or rhetorical situation in which language is used.

This is the starting point for Wordsworth's experiments. For Wordsworth, poetry and creation are forms of moral action. Our habits of mind lead to both our articulations and our actions. This educational model applies to himself as a "growing mind" and to the audience that he attempts to reach. The poet is only different from the common man by a matter of degree (he is positioned as an orator, not a prophet, at this point). As a human being, his aim is to engage experience actively, and by way of active engagement to compose his own habits of mind, which then improve his engagement of experience. As a poet, his aim is to provide his audience with opportunities and encouragement to engage experience and to reshape their own habits of mind. His belief is that such processes of engagement, when carried out continually, lead to a state in which good thinking and speaking and action are "natural" in every encounter.

Instead of suggesting that habits be dismissed completely and replaced by reason (like Godwin), or reduced to physical reactions by scientific "method" (like Hartley), Wordsworth suggests that they be considered the baseline for all decision-making and acting, and that they be remediated by returns to perceptual experience in a continual process of tuning and broadening. *In fact, he suggests that the process of tuning and broadening can and should become a habit of mind in and of itself.*

Habits of Mind and Education in Quintilian

Quintilian's *Institutes of Oratory* 10.7, the book and chapter from which Wordsworth draws his quotation, deals with "the faculty of speaking extempore." It is the final chapter in a book that Kennedy claims is "the most famous and most read portion of Quintilian's work" (101). But Kennedy also reminds us that the subject matter of this book "is unusual in a rhetorical treatise, and ... should be viewed as an expansion of the subject" (101). Book 10 is unusual precisely because it deals not with the subject matter and logical divisions of rhetoric, but with Quintilian's ideas about composition and creativity—the very subjects that Wordsworth stressed in his poetic theory, and which have suggested for many critics that he was moving toward an expressivist and antirhetorical position.

Quintilian begins Book 10 with a chapter that treats "Reading for Improvement," proceeds through chapters treating methods of composition, meditation, and oratorical practice, and ends with this discussion of extemporary speaking, which he claims is "the richest fruit of all our study" (2: 300). This book, like all of the *Institutes*, stresses the process of education; it both outlines and embodies the cultivation of reflective habits of mind that become so deeply ingrained that the orator is always ready and capable of producing moving and well-organized spontaneous expression.

In Chapter 1 Quintilian states that the "precepts of oratory" which he has outlined in previous chapters,

> though necessary to be known, are yet insufficient to produce the full power of eloquence, unless there be united with them a certain efficient readiness, which among the Greeks is called ... 'habit.' (2: 246)

These habits are acquired by reading, writing, speaking, and meditation—by imitation, practice, and reflection that lead to creative expression and effective persuasion. Quintilian writes in Chapter 3 that "Nature has herself appointed that nothing great is to be accomplished quickly, and has ordained that difficulty should precede every work of excellence; and she has even made it a law with regard to gestation, that the larger animals are retained longer in the womb of the parent" (2: 284–5). He stresses an organic metaphor here, and the process, rather than the product, remains his focus.

Central to that process is meditation, a topic that seems quite unique in a rhetorical treatise. Quintilian treats meditation as a practice both conscious and unconscious; he claims it is always at work, it "never allows itself to be idle" (2: 298). Meditation does even more than "arrange within its circle the order of things"; it also "forms an array of words, and connects together the whole texture of a speech, with such effect, that nothing is wanting to it but to write it down" (2: 298). Defined this way, meditation encompasses all the creative elements of composition. Quintilian, with typical stress on process and patience, claims that "such power of thought" evolves gradually from practice and experience. He outlines several steps in the evolution of the powers of meditation and composition:

> In the first place, a certain form of thinking must be acquired by great practice in writing, a form which may be continually attendant on our meditations; a habit of thinking must then be gradually gained by embracing in our minds a few particulars at first, in such a way that they may be faithfully repeated; next, by additions so moderate that our task may scarcely feel itself increased, our power of conception must be enlarged, and sustained by plenty of exercise; power which in a great degree depends on memory... (2: 298–9)

In this passage, Quintilian offers a vision of composition that seems very appropriate for Wordsworth. First we must shape our minds to be responsive to our meditations; then we must acquire habits of thinking that are conducive to composition; then we must enlarge our "power of conception" gradually through use.

Wordsworth's insistence on the same principles—on responsiveness, "habits of mind," and "enlarging the mind"—is well known. And it is important to note that even though memory and premeditation are central to Quintilian's creative theory, he is careful to insist that "our premeditation" should "be made with such care that fortune, while she is unable to disappoint, may have it in her power to assist us" (2: 299); "what we meditate is not to be settled with such nicety, that room is not to be allowed for a happy conception of the moment," for a "glowing thought, suggested upon the instant" (2: 299). Creation is a labor of time, but as the orator acquires experience he can trust the promptings of the moment.

These steps in composition lead, with time, to the "richest fruit of all our study, ... the faculty of speaking extempore" (2: 300). The long labor of learning and meditation and practice bring the orator to the state of "efficient readiness" that Quintilian alluded to at the beginning of Book 10. "Our style," he asserts, "must be so formed by much and diligent composition, that even what is poured forth by us unpremeditatedly may present the appearance of having been previously written" (2: 300). And "it is habit and exercise that chiefly beget facility, and if they are intermitted, even but for a short period, not only will our fluency be diminished, but our mouth may even be closed" (2: 300). These same principles are echoed in the Preface to *Lyrical Ballads* when Wordsworth asserts that from the ability to conjure up feelings within himself and "from practice," the Poet

> has acquired a greater readiness and power in expressing what he thinks and feels, and especially those thoughts and feelings which, by his own choice, or from the structure of his own mind, arise in him without immediate external excitement. (*1802 Pref, PW* 1: 138)

Here he alludes to his "habits of meditation" as he attempts to develop a sense of purposiveness that is not limited to rational awareness and "logic." He states that

> each of them [the poems of the *Lyrical Ballads*] has a worthy *purpose*. Not that I always began to write with a distinct purpose formally conceived; but habits of meditation have, I trust, so prompted and regulated my feelings, that my descriptions of such objects as strongly excite those feelings, will be found to carry along with them a *purpose*. (*1802 Pref, PW* 1: 125,27)

Wordsworth may well have modeled this much-misunderstood early statement regarding the purposes and sources of poetry on Quintilian's discussion of extemporaneous speaking in Book 10, Chapter 7. That discussion gives great weight to spontaneous eloquence, yet stresses the fact that it can only arise in minds which have developed the right habits of mind and exercised their talents.

In Book 10, Chapter 7, Quintilian stresses the importance in extemporaneous speech of a "natural activity of mind" that not only deals consciously with the ideas currently being expressed, but also unconsciously considers and arranges the ideas that should follow. He likens this "natural activity of mind" to "a certain unreflecting and mechanical habit ... by which the hand runs on in writing, and by which the eye, in reading, sees several lines, with their turns and transitions, at once, and perceives what follows before the voice has uttered what precedes" (2: 302). Quintilian is quick to differentiate between this unconscious, spontaneous "activity of mind" and mere mindlessness, reminding us that "such habit will be of advantage to us only where the art, of which we spoke, has preceded it, so that that which is done without reflection may yet have its origin in reflection" (2: 303).

Wordsworth echoes the concepts of this passage in his Preface, developing his own habits of mind that operate "blindly and mechanically," yet arise from having "thought long and deeply" and have a "worthy purpose." His definition of poetry as the "spontaneous overflow of powerful feelings" is embedded in a careful passage stressing that such "overflow" results from good habits of mind, from discipline and experience, and that it flows outward with purpose toward the understanding of the reader. Viewing this central definition of poetry with Quintilian's chapter on extemporary speaking in mind calls elements into focus that had been ignored almost completely.

The Power of Particular Experience and Context

The power of the address to feelings rather than to reason was freely acknowledged, though deprecated as unfair, in Aristotle's *On Rhetoric*. Quintilian claims that evocation and response to "feeling," both in the orator and the audience, are the central aims of rhetoric. One of the duties of an orator, he claims in Book 6 of the *Institutes of Oratory*, is that of "influencing the minds of the judges, and of moulding and transforming them, as it were, to that disposition which we wish them to assume" (Quintilian 2: 421). Proofs are not enough to accomplish such influence; Quintilian asserts that speakers who can marshal proofs are many, "but such as can seize the attention of the judge, and lead him to whatever frame of mind he desires, forcing him to weep or feel angry as their words influence him, are but rarely to be found" (2: 421). Indeed, Quintilian writes, "proofs in our favour, it is true, may make the judge think our cause the better, but impressions on his feelings make him wish it to be the better, and what he wishes he also believes" (2: 422), and "a judge, when led away by his feelings, loses the faculty of discerning truth; he is hurried along as it were by a flood, and yields to the force of a torrent" (2: 422).

Yet despite the wording here, Quintilian never advocates immoral swaying of the feelings for the sake of furthering an unjust cause. He does not discount the value of "truth" completely; he simply subordinates it to right action. He is well known for his assertion that the orator must, by necessity, be a good man—a "vir bonus." But how can we accept his stress on the appeal to "feeling" without dismissing reason, truth, and good judgment? To do so, we must let go of our dichotomy between "feeling" on the one hand and "reason" on the other—the emotive/cognitive divide that has been so popular in 20th century psychology and literary criticism.[6] We must enter the framework offered by thinkers such as Damasio in our own century: a framework that recognizes the emotional foundations of pragmatic reasoning, judgment, and decision-making.7 Quintilian's language in the passages above—"influencing the minds," "seize the attention," "frame of mind," and "impressions on his feelings" suggests a sophisticated, complex, and useful view of the nature of "feeling"—a view which informs Wordsworth's compositions as well.

In fact, both Quintilian and Wordsworth specifically relate the rush of feelings or sensations which moves both speaker and reader to the reflection and thought that moderate those feelings and to the memories and mental images which contribute to them. In Book 10, Chapter 7, Quintilian insists that "strongly conceived thoughts and images rising fresh in the mind, bear us along with uninterrupted rapidity, when they would sometimes, if retarded by the slowness of writing, grow cool, and if put off, would never return" (2: 303). And he connects these thoughts and images with feelings in the next passage:

> Those images, therefore, to which I have alluded, and which, I observed, are called fantasiai ... by the Greeks, must be carefully cherished in our minds, and everything on which we intend to speak, every person and every question, and all the hopes and fears likely to be attendant on them, must be kept full before our view, and admitted as it were into our hearts; for it is strength of feeling combined with energy of intellect, that renders us eloquent. Hence even to the illiterate words are not wanting, if they be but roused by some strong passion. (2: 303-4)

The final sentences of this passage are the ones quoted by Wordsworth in his letter to Fox. These are important words; they reach to the center of Wordsworth's approach to life and to his poetry.

Like Quintilian, Wordsworth uses "feeling" and "passion" as central concepts that do not represent sentiment or mindless emotion. Instead they often allude to a principle of engagement, by which the speaker and the audience participate willingly in an experience which can shape the conceiving minds of all participants. In a letter to John Wilson, dated June 7, 1802, Wordsworth suggests this view of feelings:

> You have given me praise for having reflected faithfully in my poems the feelings of human nature I would fain hope that I have done so. But a great Poet ought to do more than this he ought to a certain degree to rectify men's feelings, to give them new compositions of feeling, to render their feelings more sane and permanent, in short, more consonant to nature, that is, to eternal nature, and the great moving spirit of things. He ought to travel before men occasionally as well as at their sides. (*LWDW* 355)

Not only does Wordsworth insist on a clear moral purpose for poetry here, he also expands the definition of feeling well beyond the way it is often treated. The key phrases here are "new compositions of feeling," "to render their feelings more sane and permanent," and "more consonant to nature." With these phrases, Wordsworth makes it clear that he is concerned not with momentary feelings of anger or joy or pain, but with feelings that are lasting and somehow involved with our thoughts and our way of thinking.

This construction of feeling is complicated, and limited by Wordsworth's limited vocabulary. As Wordsworth uses it, the word "feeling" points in several related directions; it cannot be defined once and for all. In the Preface to *Lyrical Ballads*, for example, Wordsworth certainly uses the term "feeling" to stand for "sense" or "perception" as well as for "emotion." And we are unlikely to appreciate the nuances of his thinking unless we accept the fact that he links feeling and thought into a continuum that can only be understood if one eliminates the Cartesian divide between body and mind. Wordsworth writes:

> our continued influxes of feeling are modified and directed by our thoughts, which are indeed the representatives of all our past feelings (*1802 Pref, PW* 1: 127)

Here he clearly does not mean "emotion" by the term feeling. He means "sensation" or "perception." And note the use of the word "representatives" here. Our thoughts represent compositions of sensations or perceptions, yet they also modify and direct our "continued influxes of feeling"—our ongoing processes of perception. If seen as "circular reasoning," this model appears confusing and illogical. But Wordsworth's writing indicates that he would have understood that thinking is what Bateson and other cybernetic theorists call a recursive system or "circuit." Indeed, thinking and mind are identified by such circuits, which allow for the recognition of "difference" and the making of a sense of identity, among other things.

Following the same epistemic lines further, Wordsworth attempts to broaden the definition of the term "feeling" to include not only emotions as such, but "frames of mind" and states of "attention"—the varying affective states of engagement with perception that we as human beings move through with time. It was evident to Wordsworth, as it is to David Bohm in our own century, that our ability to perceive and understand is limited by the freedom with which the ordering of attention can change, so as to fit the order that is to be observed. (39)

If "feeling" is defined as "the affective field within which perception takes place" and mediated by a state of nonrational readiness to engage experience (Wordsworth's "wise passiveness"), then the address to feeling is paramount in any view of discourse. Only by "seizing the attention" of a reader can we hope to move them; only by inviting them to enter a new perceptual engagement can we further their own experience, which is otherwise limited by their "pre-established codes of decision." And only by their willing participation can any new understanding emerge.

But the difficulties of *aiming* such a discourse are manifold. Just how does one "seize the attention" of a reader? This question is troubling. As writers and teachers of writing, we all know just how important a question it is. But we are also painfully aware of the difficulty of answering it systematically and clearly for ourselves and for our students. That difficulty arises from the contextual entanglements that ensue whenever we attempt to formulate methods of engaging the reader, of capturing his or her interest, and of stimulating his or her learning. The reader's frame of mind is unknown to us. Is she interested in the topic we are addressing? Must we merely address that interest, or must we actively attempt to generate it? What approach to our topic will yield both clarity and power?[8]

The answers to these questions tend to be formulated in terms of imaginative constructs of "style" and "audience." These are imaginative constructs because as individual perceivers we must intuit our "audience" and the appropriate "style" with which to reach them. We must begin with some concept of what they know already, and then attempt to work on that knowledge with our discourse. I use the phrase "work on" because that is the nature of discourse, which is fundamentally rhetorical. As authors, we can do many things if we tap into the knowledge base (feelings, ideas, beliefs) of our readers. We can reaffirm that knowledge base; we can challenge it; we can subtly reshape it. All of these things are possible in the field of relationships established among author, discourse, and reader. But the entire procedure depends on successful imaginative constructs—ideas in the mind of the author concerning the audience to be addressed and how best to frame his or her discourse to reach and influence that audience. And that means that reason, while it plays a role in the process, cannot be the limiting and guiding faculty for the author. It must be supplemented by intuition (identification with the subject of the poem, and with the supposed reader), which depends on imagination or mental imaging of 'that which does not exist to the senses.' We cannot *be* the subject of the poem; we cannot *be* the supposed reader. But, according to Wordsworth, we can generate mental images—visual, empathetic, and sensual—which enable us to identify with that subject or that reader.

Now the question arises: if the author must depend on creative imagination to generate successful discourse, where does it come from? That is one of the questions that preoccupied Wordsworth throughout most of his long life. In general, he answers that question by pointing to several sources: (1) contact with "Nature," which draws out our creative minds and provides the motive force that shapes us, (2) breadth of experience, which provides us with a wealth of images to draw on, and (3) continual refinement of our understanding. Imagination does not lend itself to a linear cause/effect analysis. Instead, it lends itself to analysis within a complex recursive model like the one now being developed in composition theory. Wordsworth answered the question of where imagination came from by intuiting a self-refining model of mind in which contextually sensitive trial and error plays as large a role as purposive rational aims. Intuition can be refined over time by continual re-mediation of experience. With each re-examination of the "audience" to be addressed comes a re-mediation of the "style" and "subjects" to be addressed. With each renewed experience of a place or a person comes a broader and more comprehensive knowing of that place or person and our relationship to it. Rational purpose emerges from the field of affect, from the field of intuited relationships, and then guides further intuitive efforts, which are then re-mediated and re-examined rationally, which yield new purposes and subjects and styles, which then guide further intuitive "tries." This model combines calibration, or "trial and error" with feedback, or rational examination and re-direction.

Wordsworth started from the position of accepting individual perception as the matrix of all meaning, and then developed in essence a theory of composition, not of poetics or writing. Composition in the sense that Wordsworth suggested includes all the complexities of perceiving and organizing perception—all the complexities of creating representations of the world in discourse that addresses and "courts" other individual perceivers.

His view of composition and the composing process can be fruitfully compared to the view of rhetoric and symbolic representation that Kenneth Burke develops in *A Rhetoric of Motives*. In it, the individual must continually create and perceive meaning by experiencing and representing/remediating experience. The individual imagination exists within larger mindlike matrices that inevitably exercise considerable influence on it. It must "make something" of the field of immediate perception within which it exists (Nature), and it must contend with cultural norms and expectations (Second Nature).

Wordsworth's project was to return to the "language of the sense"— to put language to work "making something" of immediate perceptions, no matter how routine and insignificant they seemed to be under the dictates of "second nature." He turned to "Nature" as a teacher in order to provide a way to re-mediate "second nature." In his view, the individual, and particularly the poet, must work relentlessly to slip outside the domain of "second nature"—the "pre-established codes of decision" that tend to guide our perceptions and our thinking—and into the domain of re-seeing and perceiving anew. His compositions were devoted to this enterprise, seeking to re-engage his readers with their immediate sensory world and to provoke new ways of viewing that world.

And so Wordsworth offers a self-correcting model by way of two sets of continually examined relationships—the relationship between our models and our perceptions, and the relationship between our models and the models of others. Returning to the pivotal passage from the preface, he claims that

> so, by the repetition and continuance of this act, our feelings will be connected with important subjects, till at length, if we be originally possessed of much sensibility, such habits of mind will be produced, that, by obeying blindly and mechanically the impulses of those habits, we shall describe objects, and utter sentiments, of such a nature, and in such connection with each other, that the understanding of the Reader must necessarily be in some degree enlightened, and his affections strengthened and purified. (*1802 Pref, PW* 1: 127)

Reasoning and reflection must be shaped by active perception; in turn, they must guide us in our pursuit of further perception, which then reshapes our conceptions. This process, when made into an active habit of mind, ensures that we will attain value. The thing that engages us in this habit of mind, according to Wordsworth, is pleasure. And poetry is best suited to impart it.

In a letter to John Wilson dated Jun 7, 1802, Wordsworth connects "pleasure," a term traditionally related to "feeling" and yet not subsumed by it, with thought in a significant way. He responds to Wilson's reaction to the *Lyrical Ballads*, writing

> It is plain from your letter that the pleasure which I have given you has not been blind or unthinking you have studied the poems and prove that you have entered into the spirit of them. (*LWDW* 353)

Wordsworth connects pleasure, thought, and "spirit" here in a way that seems inaccessible to the modern reader. He is not limiting pleasure to the intellectual pleasure sought by Coleridge[9], but he is also extending pleasure beyond a "blind and unthinking" principle. Pleasure seems to be a willing and thinking engagement of the feelings, a chosen participation in the experience offered by the words of the poet. It is important that the reader not simply enjoy the poems as pleasurable arrangements of words, but actually "enter into the spirit of them."

In a letter to Sara Hutchinson dated June 14, 1802, Wordsworth clarifies this view of pleasure as active, thinking participation further. He writes

> My dear Sara, it is not a matter of indifference whether you are pleased with this figure and his employment; it may be comparatively so, whether you are pleased or not with *this Poem*; but it is of the utmost importance that you should have had pleasure from contemplating the fortitude, independence, persevering spirit, and the general moral dignity of this old man's character. (*LWDW* 367)

Here he links pleasure with contemplation and stresses the importance of the experience the words attempt to capture and share rather than stressing the words ("this poem") themselves.

It would be easy to dismiss such passages as illogical ramblings, but Wordsworth's connection with Quintilian and his use of similar rhetorical concepts offers a better reading. Quintilian insists that thought and feeling are vitally interconnected. The images that we have before our mind's eye, that arise from and create our feelings, that allow us to participate in experience rather than simply observing it, are what render us eloquent. Thus eloquence and meaningfulness are not limited to men of intellect. And Quintilian goes further, saying that not only do our feelings and associated images of the mind make us eloquent, they also are the key to reaching and influencing others. In Book 6, Chapter 2, he writes that "the chief requisite, then, for moving the feelings of others, is, as far as I can judge, that we ourselves be moved" (1: 427), and to prove his point asks "for what else is the reason that mourners, when their grief is fresh at least, are heard to utter exclamations of the greatest expressiveness, and that anger sometimes produces eloquence even in the ignorant, but that there are strong sensations in them, and sincerity of feeling?" (1: 427). This passage sounds very Wordsworthian in its stress on the "sincerity of feeling" that leads to eloquence in all men.

And our imagination provides the only way for us to experience feelings that then drive our eloquence. In Book 6, Chapter 2, Quintilian asks, "by what means, it may be asked, shall we be affected, since our feelings are not in our own power?" (1: 427), and his answer is:

> What the Greeks call 'fantasiai' ... we call visiones; images by which the representations of absent objects are so distinctly represented to the mind, that we seem to see them with our eyes, and to have them before us. 30. Whoever shall best conceive such images, will have the greatest power in moving the feelings. A man of such lively imagination some call [ ], being one who can vividly represent to himself things, voices, actions, with the exactness of reality; and this faculty may readily be acquired by ourselves if we desire it" (1: 427).

This passage bears a striking resemblance to Wordsworth's description of the Poet in his Preface to *Lyrical Ballads*:

> He is a man speaking to men: a man, it is true, endowed with more lively sensibility, more enthusiasm and tenderness, who has a greater knowledge of human nature, and a more comprehensive soul, than are supposed to be common among mankind; a man pleased with his own passions and volitions, and who rejoices more than other men in the spirit of life that is in him; delighting to contemplate similar volitions and passions as manifested in the goings-on of the Universe, and habitually impelled to create them where he does not find them. To these qualities he has added a disposition to be affected more than other men by absent things as if they were present; an ability of conjuring up in himself passions, which are indeed far from being the same as those produced by real events, yet (especially in those parts of the general sympathy which are pleasing and delightful) do more nearly resemble the passions produced by real events, than anything which, from the motions of their own minds merely, other men are accustomed to feel in themselves;—whence, and from practice, he has acquired a greater readiness and power in expressing what he thinks and feels, and especially those thoughts and feelings which, by his own choice, or from the structure of his

own mind, arise in him without immediate external excitement" (*1802 Pref, PW* 1: 138).

As with Quintilian, he stresses the writer's ability to "conjure up images" that are nearly as vital and convincing as the "real events themselves." The thing that sets the writer apart from most men is his "sensitivity" and "practice" which lead to "a greater readiness and power in expressing what he thinks and feels." The imagination of the writer, fed by experience and reflection on experience (meditation), reaches a state of "readiness" which allows spontaneous expression of feelings. And that spontaneous expression of feelings is what facilitates the participation of others in a process that alters their conceptions. Pleasure is both the invitation to and the result of a connection between author and reader—the joining which makes thoughtful expression rhetorically effective. The art arises from nature by way of habits of mind and long practice, and the words address themselves to the mind of the reader by way of images that are attached to feelings and thoughts.

And so it seems that Wordsworth aspires to a rhetoric like that of Quintilian—a private rhetoric that begins with individual feelings and habits of mind rather than a public rhetoric that begins with public knowledge and reason. His theory suggests that poetry, like the eloquence of Quintilian, can help to change the composition of other minds by leading them to the feelings and the habits of mind that the poet has worked to acquire. Wordsworth reminds us that

> Aristotle, I have been told, has said, that Poetry is the most philosophic of all writing: it is so: its object is truth, not individual and local, but general, and operative; not standing upon external testimony, but carried alive into the heart by passion; truth which is its own testimony, which gives competence and confidence to the tribunal to which it appeals, and receives them from the same tribunal. (*1802 Pref, PW* 1: 139)

Like Quintilian, Wordsworth connects thoughts and images and feelings in a process that unites the speaker, the spoken, and the "tribunal." And like Quintilian, Wordsworth stresses constructed reality rather than absolute "Truth." Meaning is made, not found, and yet meaning is already present all around us. This is the paradox that informs Wordsworth's work. If we listen to our experience well, then we can make meaning well, half-creating and half-perceiving. But only with disciplined engagement, or "long intercourse," can we do so. It is our disciplined engagement, on the one hand, and our relationship with larger processes in the social and natural and symbolic worlds, on the other, which maintain our thinking and our moral action in what Bateson calls "homeostasis"—a self-correcting and harmonious system. And poetry can be a means to these ends.

Chapter 8
Poetry and Composing

> ...thought with totality as its content has to be considered as an art form, like poetry, whose function is primarily to give rise to a new perception, and to action that is implicit in this perception, rather than to communicate reflective knowledge of 'how everything is.'
> —David Bohm, *Wholeness and the Implicate Order*

> '...the man I call wise is he who, for any of us to whom experiences seem and are without value, causes them by means of a change to seem and be dowered with value'
> —Protagoras, quoted in Mario Untersteiner, *The Sophists*

The earlier chapters of this text have made it possible for us to step outside Cartesian dualisms by reclaiming some rhetorical principles of knowing. With these principles in our "habits of mind," we can articulate some of the basic assumptions that underlie Wordsworth's poetic experiments. These include the following:

1. Epistemologically speaking, we cannot concern ourselves with a so-called "reality" which exists prior to our symbolic representations, which are both biological and linguistic. We *can*, however, concern ourselves with the symbolic representations themselves and with the processes by which we create them. The business of the poet, and of poetry, is to deal with what "seems" and what "appears to be." That does not by any means reduce poetry's value; in fact it asserts that poetic processes are the originators of all knowing of value.
2. Individual perception is the matrix within which all meaning is made, and so individual perception is the point of address for change.
3. Individuals are connected to other individuals and to nature not by universal "concepts" or models that provide final clarifications, but by universal structures of mind and by the human predicament, which is to suffer and die within the field of

unknowing.
4. Processes of knowing are corrected and balanced and "tuned" by engagement (rather than sequestration), practice, and a stance of openness rather than a search for closure.

Equipped with these assumptions, we can no longer read Wordsworth as if his poetry and theory are, or should be, expressions of an underlying philosophical system. This chapter will argue that we are better informed when we read Wordsworth's compositions as embodiments of his fundamentally *rhetorical* struggle to (1) organize the world into meaningful "patterns which connect," and (2) involve others in the process of finding, making and sustaining those patterns. It was no mistake for his executors to call his magnum opus *The Prelude*; he was tentative and knew he was learning as he went. He did not have the complete edifice of thought prepared before writing. On the contrary, the writing continually influenced and reshaped the edifice of thought. His continuing revisions were not primarily the result of worrisome attention to detail, but evidence of his own sense that perceptions and conceptions must always change and grow to stay alive. And he never set out to practice using a clearly developed *a priori* theory. Even as he writes he struggles—and invites others to struggle—with meaning, with value, and with issues of relationship and identity.

Within this rhetorical framework, we can come to terms with some of the complications of Wordsworth's definitions and uses of poetry. The term "Poetry," as Wordsworth uses it in the evolving Prefaces to *Lyrical Ballads*, emphasizes mental processes rather than the characteristics of literary objects. In theory and practice, Wordsworth shows that poetry is a *process* of mind to be entered and participated in, rather than a product to be admired. Poetry is to be an *extension* of experience rather than a crystallization or an explanation of experience in language. His poetry can be seen as the embodiment of two simultaneous rhetorical processes—the effort to capture powerful experience in language, and the effort to generate powerful experience using language—and two complementary modes—participatory and reflective.

But these processes and modes exist in a connected continuum, and cannot be abstracted from each other. Individual poems often represent both processes and use both modes of representation/rhetoric. And everything is complicated further by Wordsworth's purposeful blurring of the convenient lines that discourse theorists such as Abrams and Kinneavy have drawn between expressive and persuasive uses of language.[1] His rhetorical approach centers on what Kenneth Burke calls "identification"—the rhetorical stance that seeks to merge the expressive and persuasive functions of discourse—and on what he saw as the universal structure of mental processes that would allow such identification, rather than on rational structures of "thinking" and traditional "figures" of language and logic. As a result, his poems are often rich experiences and poor sources of philosophical clarity—as they should be.

Wordsworth's Rhetorical Stance

How did Wordsworth attempt to realize his fundamentally democratic, perception-centered vision for poetry? And how did he hope to change his culture's "pre-established codes of decision"? His rhetorical plan, in its broad outline, was to address and move a broad and diverse audience toward more comprehensive thinking. And his rhetorical "stance" was experimental and emergent.

Lynette Hunter establishes some helpful ground rules for examining rhetorical "stances" in her book *Rhetorical Stance in Modern Literature*. Rhetorical stance, she argues, is not to be understood as 'a position taken towards the subject matter of an argument' (static), but as an evolving position meant to facilitate meetings of minds (dynamic). According to Hunter, *stance*

> brings together what is written with the writer and the reader. It provides the meeting-place for all three that in practice makes them inseparable. (6)

This means that stance is not—cannot be—an entirely purposive construction. Instead it must be seen as an emergent function of the processes of composition. Stance, then, depends heavily on Bateson's "calibration." Only by experimenting, trying on new positions, attempting to reach readers on their own terms, to identify with them in order to change them, can one find the appropriate rhetorical stance. When discussing Chesterton's political rhetoric, Hunter describes a pattern very much like the one that Wordsworth tried to establish. She writes that Chesterton

> tried to provide for a positive political rhetoric [against the negative propagandized rhetoric of Hitler] which he based on the opposing forces of public discussion and continual reassessment. The two go hand in hand for reassessment is not possible without variety of opinion, open disagreement and an education in different values ... Assessment makes necessary self-criticism, correction, and reconstruction, and is based on a constant examination of assumptions. With criticism goes education which needs explanation, attention to fact, and the need for a common policy. The two depend on personal conviction, mental activity, and choice. Their constant reassessment of value makes the rhetoric overt, and may lead to charges of inconsistency. However, the fundamental consistency underlying the surface is a long-term rhetorical strategy which should gain increasing respect and adherence. (18)

This idea of a long-term rhetorical purpose, centering on continual re-evaluation and re-assessment, fits Wordsworth's compositions well. As Hewitt (*Empirical Dilemma*) claims, Wordsworth tries many different approaches to his readers. But he also challenges them to carry on "a constant examination of their assumptions" by exposing them to situations that they are unfamiliar with and encouraging them to identify with characters that they would normally fail even to perceive. Wordsworth's particular rhetorical approaches are many, but his broad rhetorical stance is coherent and unified.

That rhetorical stance is quite sophisticated, even fairly early in his career. It is founded on openness rather than closure (my writing is "experimental"; it is not these particular poems and their views, but the principles upon which they are written, which really matter). It does not assert absolute values, but stresses the process of self-conscious, well-considered value making. It accepts the incompleteness of knowledge and rational exposition, and insists on the necessity of recursiveness: reassessment is built into the rhetorical model, and founds the "philosophy." It stresses identification and engagement both between author and "subject" and between reader and "text." It courts popular appeal and democratization of authority: "The language of men, not poets." And it acknowledges its dependence on the reader's fair judgment: gives confidence to, and receives validation from, the "tribunal" of real human beings that judge it.

Built into his developing stance is an awareness of the slipperiness of language and the necessity of a rhetorical "vector" whenever language is used. Wordsworth's paradoxes (Clarke) and his stress on "feeling" and "passion" are evidence of this element. Wordsworth was always aware, as was Quintilian, that belief and conviction are grounded in shared "feeling" (non-rational mindfulness), and that all rhetorical appeals must engage it. Wordsworth does not limit himself to hierarchical and linear thinking, so he chooses multivalence (even at the cost of being considered "inconsistent") rather than uniformity.

All in all, Wordsworth's rhetorical plan was to compose in ways that demand and facilitate active engagement in processes of mind rather than relying on "pre-established codes of decision." And by doing so, he sought to encourage the gradual calibration, the gradual broadening of knowing that emerges from "long intercourse" with valuable experiences and ideas. This plan allows for both incremental change—calibration—which emerges from the reader's encounter with the entire body of his work over time, and the sudden transformations and insights that only moving experience can bring.

Wordsworth's View of "Poetry"

"Poetry," for many readers, is a set of expectations. Expectations about metric and spatial form, about subject matter, about modes of treatment. In other words, "Poetry" is a concept.

Wordsworth recognized this, and berated his predecessors of the eighteenth century for treating "Poetry-as-concept" as if it were the sum total of what "Poetry" IS. In the original "Advertisement" to the Lyrical Ballads, he asks his readers to throw away their expectations about "Poetry" and to *experience* his writing before attempting to judge it. He writes:

> It is desirable that ... readers, for their own sakes, should not suffer the solitary word Poetry, a word of very disputed meaning, to stand in the way of their gratification; but that, while they are perusing this book, they should ask themselves if it contains a natural delineation of human passions, human characters, and human incidents; and if the answer be favorable to the author's wishes, that they should consent to be pleased in spite of that most dreadful enemy to our pleasures, our own pre-established codes of decision. (*Adv, PW* 1: 116)

When reading this passage, it is all too easy to make the assumption that Wordsworth is substituting a new set of "rules and regulations" about poetry. If we are stuck at the level of "Poetry-as-concept," there is no other way to respond to this passage.

We have done Wordsworth a great injustice by reading him this way. The result of such a position is to treat him as an inspired poet but a muddleheaded thinker (since he writes beautiful poems, but claims an originality that he may or may not really live up to, and since he never provides us with the clearly-defined new conceptual "system" of poetry that we expect from him).

What Wordsworth says in this passage is not complicated, yet it is hardly ever taken seriously. He simply says, "Look. Don't confuse yourself with definitions and expectations of what poetry ought to be; simply enjoy the experience of these poems! If you see in them people, events, and feelings that move you, then be moved. Treat them as experiences, not as aesthetic objects for analysis."

Wordsworth's "revolutionary" step was to insist that "Poetry" should be seen first and foremost as "the process of (sharing) perception" rather than as "the product of Art." Once this is understood, many of his complicated positions and definitions become coherent and meaningful. He wishes to *move* his readers, to *engage* them, to *involve* them. His claim that "there is no knowledge without pleasure" makes perfect sense when the affective elements of learning are included in our view.

As teachers, we all know that students learn nothing until they become involved, until they engage the experiences that we offer them, until they enter the process of learning. They may memorize facts and figures, but they aren't really learning until they are involved and interested enough to start making their own connections, to build their own networks of meaning. Wordsworth was interested in this primary pedagogical truth. He saw the development of taste and understanding and knowledge *not* as the acquisitions of certain immutable standards or sets of data, but as the gradual refinement and broadening of one's relationship with experience.

He sought to bring his readers into the process of entering new experiences fully, of wondering and participating, of absorbing and synthesizing, and of examining and considering by way of "long intercourse." The primary vehicle for doing all these things, according to

Wordsworth, was not systematic philosophy, not science, and not elegant or ornamental verse. The vehicle was poetry, which was constructed as a medium of representation and as a purpose rather than as a form. This is absolutely vital to understanding Wordsworth. He experimented with poetic forms and approaches often, but he never deviated from his *purpose* and his commitment to poetry as the vivid verbal representation of experience.

Wordsworth asserts that each of his poems in the *Lyrical Ballads*

> has a worthy purpose. Not that I mean to say, that I always began to write with a distinct purpose formally conceived; but I believe that my habits of meditation have so formed my feelings, as that my descriptions of such objects as strongly excite those feelings, will be found to carry along with them a purpose (*1802 Pref, PW* 1: 127).

In a culture where everything is rationalized and systematized, this looks like an empty or mystical statement. But it is not. If one accepts that our minds work on many levels besides the conscious rational level, if one accepts that much of our behavior is dependent on our habits of mind, and if one accepts that knowing is as much a process and a state of relationship as a set of facts and contents, then one can take Wordsworth's claim seriously here. The purpose of poetry is to represent experience in such a way as to provoke the audience into engagement with 'the other' in order to renew that audience's engagement with experience. It does not matter so much what the particular poem is, as long as the audience enters the process.

Wordsworth makes this quite clear in his letters. He says repeatedly that it is not the particular poems, but the approach and feeling and interaction that they attempt to generate, that matters. He claims in the 1800 Preface that

> it is proper that I should mention one other circumstance which distinguishes these Poems from the popular Poetry of the day; it is this, that the feeling therein developed gives importance to the action and situation and not the action and situation to the feeling. (*PW* 1: 128)

Again, we must recall the complexities of the word "feeling" as Wordsworth used it. It was probably the best word that Wordsworth could find to describe the non-rational state of relationship that he felt was so important to knowing and learning. He sees this as one of the cores of his whole program:

> I point my Reader's attention to this mark of distinction far less for the sake of these particular Poems than from the general importance of the subject. The subject is indeed important! For the human mind is capable of excitement without the application of gross and violent stimulants; and he must have a very faint perception of its beauty and dignity who does not know this, and who does not further know that one being is elevated above another in proportion as he possesses this capability. It has therefore appeared to me that to endeavour to produce or enlarge this capability is one of the best services in which, at any time, a Writer can be engaged ... (*PW* 1: 128)

Wordsworth goes on, of course, to claim that the need for this capability is even greater in his present time. I argue that he is talking specifically about the human mind's capacity to engage in connection with other minds, other experiences, and other worlds: in short, the ability to get outside one's own preconceptions and to reconnect with experience. When such engagement occurs, poetry can break down the barriers of false assumptions and help readers to broaden their experience, sympathize with others, and re-examine their lives.

"Identification" and Burke's Broader View of Rhetoric

In *A Rhetoric of Motives*, Burke extends the domain of rhetoric to include not only persuasion as such, but also what he calls "identification." Identification might fruitfully be considered as the intertwining of ethos and pathos, the point at which the character of the speaker becomes an emotional (or unconscious) appeal to the audience. Burke claims that

> You persuade a man only insofar as you can talk his language by speech, gesture, tonality, order, image, attitude, idea, identifying your ways with his. (55)

In effect, Burke suggests, the speaker moves the audience by speaking its language and entering into its concerns, by becoming "consubstantial" with it. The listeners find the speaker's appeal convincing because they participate in it; they feel as if the speaker says things that they might have said themselves. Burke reminds us that Longinus, a rhetorician who also influenced Wordsworth, "refers to that kind of elation wherein the audience feels as though it were not merely receiving, but were itself creatively participating in the poet's or speaker's assertion" (58). In Longinus' own words, the soul of the listener "takes a proud flight, and is filled with joy and vaunting, as though it had itself produced what it has heard" (65). And Burke asks the pointed question: "Could we not say that, in such cases, the audience is exalted by the assertion because it has the feel of collaborating in the assertion?" (58).

Burke suggests that such "exaltation" works rhetorically by moving the audience's feelings. It is a form of "moving" which is akin to, but different from, the rhetorical moving to decision. Transport or transformation, rather than traditional conscious persuasion, is the aim of identification. Burke writes that

> Where Demosthenes would transport his auditors the better to persuade them, Longinus treats the state of transport as the aim. Hence he seeks to convey the quality of the excitement, and to disclose the means by which it is produced. Indeed, might not his key term, that is usually translated 'sublime,' come close to what we mean by 'moving,' not in the rhetorical sense, of moving an audience to a decision, but as when we say of a poem, 'How moving!' (65).

In effect, the rhetorician starts from the ground of the audience's existing opinions and comfortable language and moves them by way of such identification to expand those opinions in new directions: "Some of their opinions are needed to support the fulcrum by which he would move other opinions" (56). The rhetor's aim is to move the audience by appealing to logos and kairos, to their existing habits of mind and the context of the moment. But by appealing to logos and kairos, the effective rhetor can enlist the audience in a re-negotiation of logos itself. When attended to, kairos always injects the unknown and the particular into the field of universal symbolic constructions. The rhetor harnesses that force and channels it into a reshaping of the logos—a "power" that can move the audience toward new "habits of mind."

By broadening the range of rhetorical appeal and action, Burke's principle of identification provides a helpful entry into the study of Wordsworth's rhetorical purposes. It asserts that the speaker must enter into a pact with the audience by speaking their language and starting from accepted opinions; it reminds us that rhetoric can be addressed to "attitude" as well as specific "action"; and it removes the classical limitation of rhetoric to deliberate conscious design, enabling us to view the "moving" aspects of poetry as forms of rhetorical appeal. In effect, Wordsworth weds oratory to poetics by way of the moving force of "pleasure"—a valid technique that Burke discusses in *A Rhetoric of Motives*. He does not aim to teach or instruct by way of "formally conceived" purposes, but he does aim to move his audience by way of pleasure.

Poetic "Pleasure" as a Form of "Identification"

Wordsworth's use of the term "pleasure" is little discussed, but it is absolutely central to his poetic theory. In the Preface, it obviously means more than aesthetic pleasure divorced from "moral relations" and real life considerations. Wordsworth claims that

> the pleasure which I have proposed to myself to impart, is of a kind very different from that which is supposed by many persons to be the proper object of poetry. (*1802 Pref, PW* 1: 131)

He articulates a view of pleasure that connects the term with the broader concept of "rational sympathy"—which, like Burke's "identification," is the principle that connects us to the things that we care about. Wordsworth writes that

> We have no sympathy but what is propagated by pleasure: I would not be misunderstood; but whereever we sympathize with pain, it will be found ever that the sympathy is produced and carried on by subtle combinations with pleasure. We have no knowledge, that is, no general principles drawn from the contemplation of particular facts, but what has been built up by pleasure, and exists in us by pleasure alone. (*1802 Pref, PW* 1: 140)

Thus pleasure depends on a willing engagement with the subject of our contemplation; it is, for Wordsworth, the principle that enables him to "excite rational sympathy" (*1802 Pref, PW* 1: 143) in his readers.

The "rational sympathy" which Wordsworth aims to evoke depends not only on identification with his readers—by addressing them in their own language and treating issues with which they are concerned—but also with the subjects of his poetry. He claims that "it will be the wish of the Poet to bring his feelings near to those of the persons whose feelings he describes, nay, for short spaces of time, perhaps, to let himself slip into an entire delusion, and even confound and identify his feelings with theirs" (*1802 Pref, PW* 1: 138). In short, his poetic theory centers on the participation of both author and reader in a potentially transforming experience.2

Poetry is the expression of a moving experience of interaction, and the Poem then becomes in and of itself the site of another moving experience of interaction. Poetry both represents and participates in processes of mindfulness. It is a principle of relationship, by way of which the author engages reality and the reader engages the author's experience of reality that in turn becomes part of his or her experience of reality.

This is why Wordsworth was so concerned with feeling and empathy and "rational sympathy." "Power," for him, was the element that made discourse moving, that established a ground of connection between author and reader and represented experience. True to his view that participation and reflection were a continuum, and his placement of poetry in that continuum, his poetic approaches sometimes reflected on processes of mind, sometimes embodied them, and sometimes simply attempted to provoke them. In his efforts to encourage both participation and reflection, Wordsworth used a number of strategies, four of which might be described as follows:

1. *Unfamiliar identification.* This strategy, which informs poems such as "The Mad Mother" and "The Idiot Boy," places the reader in the position of having to identify with people or experiences that were unfamiliar to them. This is the most risky rhetorical strategy because it relies heavily on the reader's willing participation in an experience that would normally be shunned as stupid or insignificant or unimportant. Byron's response to "The Idiot Boy" in "English Bards and Scotch Reviewers" shows that even a highly perceptive reader could easily "miss the point."
2. *Mixed identification.* This strategy, which informs the Matthew poems, "We are Seven," and many others, invites the reader to enter the process of knowing by facing and identifying with several viewpoints. The reader is encouraged not to accept one viewpoint, but to engage the multiple viewpoints in the poem.

Mental process is engaged by the refusal of easy answers. The reader must resolve the complications of difference in his or her own terms.

3. *Shared Re-evaluation.* "The Solitary Reaper," "A Night-Piece," and "The Thorn" are poems that show a more self-conscious attention to the workings of Wordsworth's model of knowing. These poems sketch out, and invite participation in, the movement from predisposition to sudden awareness of new context to assimilation of/reflection on new context.

4. *Reflection on Re-evaluation.* "Tintern Abbey" and *The Two-Part Prelude* represent Wordsworth's most self-conscious strategies. Here Wordsworth attempts to capture the processes of mind as he knows them and to reveal them to the reader through his own experiences (not didactically, but in the embodiment of participation and reflection).

Wordsworth developed and tried many ways to reach his readers, knowing that no plan for doing so could be 'foolproof.' All of his poems were self-consciously "experimental," and his hope was that the body of his compositions would reach his audience—if not this particular poem, then some other poem. But Wordsworth believed that a reader had to enter into the structure of the entire body of his compositions in order to broaden their understanding and judgment about the individual poems and the meaning they represented. I will address several examples here and then leave you to engage the others with new "habits of mind."

"We are Seven"

Wordsworth's rhetorical effort to use "mixed identification" as a means for altering the reader's attitude can be seen at work in poems such as "We are Seven." This little poem, written in simple and direct language, reveals the extraordinary nature of an ordinary situation by involving the reader in a double identification with its characters. If examined with the prevailing standards of (Neo)classical rhetoric in mind, the poem seems completely free of rhetorical purpose. It makes no effort to stimulate action in the reader; it does not "take a side" and attempt to persuade by argument; it simply cannot be seen as an attempt to resolve difference by way of verbal power. But it has rhetorical motives that Kenneth Burke would recognize: by way of identification it seeks to resolve difference into an overarching unity, moving to a higher level of generality in which both sides are "right."

Wordsworth begins the poem with a general question that invites us as readers to enter a sympathetic and protective frame of mind before meeting the specific little girl of the story to unfold:

> —— A SIMPLE Child,
> That lightly draws its breath,
> And feels its life in every limb,
> What should it know of death? (*PoW* 66)

The language of this stanza appeals to our memory of being young and "simple" and full of "life," of being unburdened and free of the worries of adulthood. It encourages us to identify with the child's interests by asking a question of value—What should such a child know of death?—rather than a question of fact—what would such a child know? The general issues treated and the formulation of the question at hand—of course such an innocent little child should know nothing of death—encourage us to assume a sympathetic and protective stance toward any innocent child.

That stance is strengthened and focused by the detailed description of the "little cottage Girl" which follows in the second and third stanzas. As readers, we are encouraged to join in the narrator's feeling—"Her beauty made me glad"—by the details of her charm, her "rustic" simplicity, her eyes which are "fair—and very fair" (*PoW* 66). By accepting the general claim of innocent children to sympathy and protection, and by participating in the narrator's experience, we come to identify with this particular little girl.

But when the narrator speaks, he separates himself from the little girl with a series of questions:

> "Sisters and brothers, little Maid,
> How many may you be?"
> "How many? Seven in all," she said,
> And wondering looked at me.
>
> "And where are they? I pray you tell."
> She answered, "Seven are we;

> And two of us at Conway dwell,
> And two are gone to sea.
>
> "Two of us in the church-yard lie,
> My sister and my brother;
> And, in the church-yard cottage, I
> Dwell near them with my mother." (*PoW* 66)

The girl gives what she considers to be a straightforward account of her family situation in response to the man's questions. But her account does not satisfy the narrator, who takes a more literal-minded approach:

> "You say that two at Conway dwell,
> And two are gone to sea,
> Yet ye are seven! I pray you tell,
> Sweet Maid, how this may be." (*PoW* 66)

This response opens a rhetorical dialectic between the man and the girl in which each offers an interpretation of the facts and attempts to persuade the other to accept that interpretation.

The girl accounts for her two dead siblings again; the man insists that if they are dead then only five siblings remain. Any reader who has reached a sympathetic identification with the girl in the opening stanzas cannot simply reject her poignant claims:

> "Their graves are green, they may be seen,"
> The little Maid replied,
> "Twelve steps or more from my mother's door,
> And they are side by side.
>
> "My stockings there I often knit,
> My kerchief there I hem;
> And there upon the ground I sit,
> And sing a song to them. (*PoW* 66)

Her brother and sister remain a part of her life, a part of her mental landscape, and her touching words remind us of the power of memory to maintain the image of our loved ones for years after their death.

As rational readers, however, we cannot wholly refuse the logic of the man either. His exasperation at the end of the poem may seem silly, but we understand it completely:

> "But they are dead; those two are dead!
> Their spirits are in heaven!"
> 'Twas throwing words away; for still
> The little Maid would have her will,
> And said, "Nay, we are seven!" (*PoW* 66)

The effect of such a double identification—of "feeling" with the little girl and of rational understanding with the man—encourages the participating reader not to accept one interpretation or the other as "right," but to resolve the dialectic by recognizing the general truths about perception which their interaction reveals. Both of their interpretations represent valid perceptual positions: the two that are dead remain present in memory and in the emotional life of the little girl despite their indubitable physical absence, yet in the broader view of an outsider the two are completely inaccessible.

Like many of Wordsworth's best poems, "We are Seven" uses the rhetorical appeal of simple descriptive language in an effort to create sympathetic identification with its characters. This particular poem creates identification with divergent views, encouraging the reader to enter, and perhaps synthesize, a complex dialectic rather than "choosing a side."

"Tintern Abbey"

"Tintern Abbey" is a manifesto and an embodiment of Wordsworth's rhetorical epistemology. In it, the poet invites the reader to both recognize and continue his own processes of making meaning. The structure of the poem embodies and invites connections and relationships—between the poet's past and present views, between the landscape and his mind, between his mind and his sister's mind, and between any one mind and other minds. It is a poem of ongoing process, of new engagement, of return and revision. It is a poem about Wordsworth's Ecology of Mind.

From the first lines, which refer to "These waters rolling from their mountain-springs / With a sweet inland murmur" (*Pedlar* 33), Wordsworth uses two of his central metaphors of mind to associate the living world around him with his own reflection and personal growth. *Water*, which represents the blending of many sources into a moving identity, and *music*, which represents the blending of diverse moving tonal threads into a living structure of sound, are two of the central metaphors that Wordsworth uses here and elsewhere to represent life and mental process: "the pattern which connects." In fact, The Prelude begins with the river Derwent, and interweaves his relations with that river into his account of the growth of his own mind. He states outright there that "The mind of man is fashioned and built up / Even as a strain of music" (*Pedlar* 43).

Wordsworth invites identification here in at least two ways. He opens the poem with "Five years have passed, five summers, with the length / Of five long winters..." (*Pedlar* 33), beginning with a universal of mental process—the awareness of the often-weary passage of time. And he writes about a return to a place, and an experience, that meant something to him. The elegiac tone invites us to value and participate in his vision as if it were our own. And it could be. We all have places and events in our lives that hold a particular place of power and meaningfulness. By example, he invites us to reflect on those places and events, and to reconsider what they mean to us.

It is critical to recognize that people are a part of this landscape. This is no secluded view of "Nature" free of human intervention. The persona views "plots of cottage-ground" and "orchard-tufts," "hedge-rows" and "pastoral farms," as well as "these steep and lofty cliffs, / Which on a wild secluded scene impress / Thoughts of more deep seclusion, and connect / The landscape with the quiet of the sky." The connections are being made here, not just between poet and landscape, and between landscape and "sky," but between the worlds of human arts and natural processes. The full passage from which the human elements cited above emerge reads as follows:

> The day is come when I again repose
> Here under this dark sycamore, and view
> These plots of cottage-ground, these orchard-tufts
> Which at this season, with their unripe fruits,
> Among the woods and copses lose themselves,
> Nor with their green and simple hue disturb
> The wild green landscape. Once again I see
> These hedge-rows—hardly hedge-rows, little lines
> Of sportive wood run wild—these pastoral farms
> Green to the very door ... (*Pedlar* 33)

The human elements exist in harmony with, and to some extent subordinate to, the larger natural processes that surround them. The "cottage-ground" and "orchard-tufts" "lose themselves" among the "woods and copses"; their "green and simple hue" is united with the "wild green landscape." The "hedge-rows" are not fence-like assaults on the living landscape, but "little lines / Of sportive wood run wild." The "pastoral farms" are "Green to the very door"; like everything else, they are integrated with the "wild green landscape." Physical presence and mental process are also integrated. Wordsworth paints a view of the landscape, and the human elements within it, that we can recognize today as a balanced ecosystem. And he does so by purposeful selection and composition, choosing not to address the evidence of industrialization that could be seen just south of him along the river Wye. He seeks to show what ought to be and what could be, not what was beginning to seem inevitable.

After establishing his complex sense of integration and relationship, and attempting to forge a bond of reflective identification with his readers, Wordsworth attempts to engage the reader in the act of placing a value on experience. He illustrates the way that participation in, and memory of, such moments of harmony and integration—"these forms of beauty"—can enrich and inform one's life on both conscious and unconscious levels:

> oft, in lonely rooms, and mid the din
> Of towns and cities, I have owed to them
> In hours of weariness sensations sweet
> Felt in the blood, and felt along the heart,
> And passing even into my purer mind
> With tranquil restoration—feelings too
> Of unremembered pleasure: such, perhaps,
> As may have had no trivial influence
> On that best portion of a good man's life,
> His little nameless unremembered acts
> Of kindness and of love. (*Pedlar* 34)

This passage embodies and shows the working of Wordsworth's connection between feeling and thinking. The harmony and beauty of the landscape are "felt in the blood, and felt along the heart," eventually passing into the "purer mind." Wordsworth attempts to describe the continuum between the physical engagement of the landscape, the "forms of beauty" that it offers the mind during that engagement, the "sensations sweet" felt by the beholder later, and the thoughts and actions that emerge from the entire process. Moments like this one shape our habits of mind; if they are moments of harmony and joy and beauty, they will blend together into a "strain of music" that will be balanced and beautiful. Wordsworth stresses the habitual nature of good action—the unconsciousness of it—in his repetition of "unremembered." The line which cites "The best portion of a good man's life" echoes with Quintilian's conviction that the orator should be "the good man speaking [and by implication acting] well."

It is interesting that Wordsworth calls the rooms "lonely" and characterizes "towns and cities" using the term "din"—which is opposed to harmonious music. And his movement in the rest of this passage is toward a recognition of the difference between sacred participation in Nature and tired repetition of Second Nature. To the "forms of beauty," he claims,

> I may have owed another gift,
> Of aspect more sublime: that blessed mood
> In which the burthen of the mystery,
> In which the heavy and the weary weight
> Of all this unintelligible world,
> Is lightened—that serene and blessed mood
> In which the affections gently lead us on,
> Until, the breath of this corporeal frame
> And even the motion of our human blood
> Almost suspended, we are laid asleep
> In body and become a living soul,
> While, with an eye made quiet by the power
> Of harmony and the deep power of joy,
> We see into the life of things.
> (*Pedlar* 35)

Wordsworth resorts to the old dichotomy between body and soul here, but the drift is toward the unity of individual mind and larger mind—a moment of participating consciousness. We are not separate and discrete bodily entities in such a moment, but living parts of a larger moving whole. Wordsworth's belief is that only experiences like this one—in which nature, culture, and the individual human mind are integrated into a larger harmony—can provide us with the ability to feel sacredness and value, to "see into the life of things."

He does not claim to *know* that his experiences at Tintern Abbey have formed his ability to experience "that blessed mood," but to *feel* it as truth. He has turned to the river Wye repeatedly as a corrective for "the fretful stir / Unprofitable and the fever of the world" (*Pedlar* 35), because he sees the Wye as a better model of mind and value. Like the river Derwent in *The Prelude*, the Wye is a "beauteous stream" that makes "ceaseless music through the night and day." Wordsworth's ecology of mind depends on natural processes like the river, which

> with its steady cadence tempering
> Our human waywardness, composed my thoughts
> To more than infant softness, giving me
> Among the fretful dwellings of mankind
> A knowledge, a dim earnest, of the calm
> Which Nature breathes ... (*Pedlar* 41)

He does not claim to have factual knowledge of the relationships he attempts to establish, yet he has faith that these relationships do exist and are meaningful.

And now, the landscape exists for him both as a physical engagement and as a "picture in the mind" which is even as he speaks being reshaped and revived. This is the cause of both "somewhat of a sad perplexity" and a "pleasure," because it reminds him both of the loss of his earlier experience of the landscape and the fact that "in this moment there is life and food / For future years." Renewed experiences, and the resulting "pictures in his mind" will once again provide him with "sensations sweet" in his daily life. He sees the landscape differently now, and he sees himself differently because of that different vision. His experience of the landscape as a younger man was one of complete participating consciousness—of "aching joys" and "dizzying raptures"—and now he returns to reflect on the landscape, its value to him, and his own changes. And so the poem is, to some extent, about loss.

But while that time [of immediacy and participation in Nature's processes] "is past," the persona claims:

> Not for this
> Faint I, nor mourn, nor murmur: other gifts
> Have followed, for such loss, I would believe,
> Abundant recompense.
> (*Pedlar* 37)

It is important to note that he does feel strongly the loss of continuing participation, of immediacy, of oneness with Nature, of a "feeling and a love / That had no need of a remoter charm / By thought supplied, or any interest / Unborrowed from the eye" (*Pedlar* 36). This immediacy is what he senses that his culture lacks, and he insists that we must return to it at least in memory, and in experience whenever possible, to find value. Yet he "would believe" that "other gifts" have followed—gifts of reflection and of awareness more comprehensive than that possible in a world of "glad animal movements." And the remainder of the poem, with all its power, focuses on these "other gifts" and the way that they complete his representation-centered view of knowing.

Framed by Wordsworth's effort to see the world as an ecology of mind and to stress the universals of mental processes and habits as a ground for identification between poet and reader, the remainder of the poem becomes not a vague projecting of his own mind into nature and his sister, but a continuing representation of central connections and their value. The sublime passage that follows indicates that he has felt the presence of Nature as a larger mind, and that he sees his engagement with Nature as the source of moral understanding. The connections, the living web, the "pattern which connects" includes both "Nature" and the "still sad music of humanity" which is always part of nature. And it is only through the perception of these connections that we can have "lofty thoughts"—a recognition of "all the mighty world / Of eye and ear, both what they half-create / And what perceive" (*Pedlar* 38). Immediate participation is powerful and rich, but we must have reflection, thought, and imagination to see "differences that make a difference," to make beauty and value and share them with others.

And sharing is Wordsworth's central concern in the final section of the poem. Here he creates new recursive connections, between his own experiences and reflections, his utterances about them, and his sister's experiences and reflections-to-be. He sees that his sister's experience of the landscape is like his own at that earlier stage in his life five years ago:

> in thy voice I catch
> The language of my former heart, and read
> My former pleasures in the shooting lights
> Of thy wild eyes. Oh, yet a little while
> May I behold in thee what I was once,

> My dear, dear sister. (*Pedlar* 39)

Through her, he recaptures the feeling of immediate participation that he had earlier. In her, he sees at work the processes of mind on which he is currently reflecting. With her, he both shares and embodies his vision of the value of experience and mental process. His poem, he hopes, will be a source of strength and beauty for her in later years, as the immediate experience of the landscape has been for him and is for her now:

> If solitude, or fear, or pain, or grief,
> Should be thy portion, with what healing thoughts
> Of tender joy wilt thou remember me
> And these my exhortations. (*Pedlar* 40)

The poem itself, the moment captured in language, has now become a part of Dorothy's field of experience. She can return to it, as she can return to the Abbey itself, to renew her sense of the value of experience. It is in this spirit that the poem closes with Wordsworth's statement that his return to the landscape near Tintern Abbey, and his vision of that landscape were more dear "both for themselves, and for thy sake." The act of sharing that return, that vision, that experience, is central to the meaning of the poem. The reader is invited, like Dorothy, to engage the landscape, too, and to participate in the process of reflecting on its meaningfulness and value. The process continues outside the bounds of the poem, and is sustained by the poem itself as a representation of a process of mind.

"The Solitary Reaper"

"The Solitary Reaper" beautifully embodies Wordsworth's ongoing invitation to his readers to join him in mindful processes. This poem embodies poesis—or meaning-making—in several concrete contexts: (1) the reaper finding and making value in her daily labor, both in the cutting and binding of the grain and the singing of her "melancholy strain," (2) the persona finding and making value in his experience of the reaper's song and his reflection on it, (3) the reader finding and making value in the experience of the poem and his/her reflection on it, and (4) the act of finding and making value in any situation.

It begins by encouraging us, as readers, to join the persona in an experience:

> Behold her, single in the field,
> Yon solitary Highland Lass!
> Reaping and singing by herself;
> Stop here, or gently pass!
> Alone she cuts and binds the grain,
> And sings a melancholy strain;
> O listen! for the Vale profound
> Is overflowing with the sound.

"Behold her ..." and "Stop here, or gently pass!" and "O listen!" are all words of invitation: words intended to secure our affective participation. As we enter the field of the poem, the persona is describing the woman in terms of isolation: she is "single," "solitary," "by herself," "alone." But the movement of the remainder of the poem shows us that the woman is not actually as isolated as the initially seems to be. The music connects her to her work, to the field she works in, and to her listeners—including us. In effect, the acts of singing and listening overcome the original isolation of reaper, persona, and ourselves as readers, uniting us in a dance of perception.

The first stanza closes with the claim that "the Vale profound / Is overflowing with the sound" of her song. Her music is not a wispy thread of creative expression in a workaday world. Instead it is abundantly present, tied intimately with her work of cutting and binding the grain, and meaningful as a connective tissue for everything else in the poem. It is, in Bateson's terms, "the pattern which connects." The second stanza continues this movement by broadening the connections made:

> No Nightingale did ever chaunt
> More welcome notes to weary bands
> Of travellers in some shady haunt,
> Among Arabian sands:
> A voice so thrilling ne'er was heard
> In spring-time from the Cuckoo-bird,
> Breaking the silence of the seas
> Among the farthest Hebrides.

The reaper's song, as song, is connected to the melodies of Nightingales in Arabia and Cuckoos in the isles off Scotland. From one end of the earth to the other, from high to low, from wet to dry and hot to cold, song and music (and poetry) connect us to one another.

Those connections extend though time as well as space, joining past, present, and future:

> Will no one tell me what she sings?—
> Perhaps the plaintive numbers flow
> For old, unhappy, far-off things,
> And battles long ago:
> Or is it some more humble lay,
> Familiar matter of today?
> Some natural sorrow, loss, or pain,
> That has been, and may be again?

It does not matter nearly as much *what* she sings as *that* she sings. The persona cannot tell what she sings, but surmises that it might equally well be a song of "old, unhappy, far-off things, / And battles long ago" or a "more humble lay, / Familiar matter of today?" But in either case, it is the act of singing that transcends the "matter" and places the reaper in contact with the persona and the reader. The song, like all processes of human creativity, transcends time and space to connect us one to the other:

> Whate'er the theme, the Maiden sang
> As if her song could have no ending;
> I saw her singing at her work,
> And o'er the sickle bending;—
> I listened, motionless and still;
> And, as I mounted up the hill,
> The music in my heart I bore,
> Long after it was heard no more.

The primary connection is established by the acts of singing and of listening, two acts that enable human beings to make meaning through creative mindful processes. It is the processes and structures of mind, and our common lot as folk who must live and die in the realm of unknowing, that connect us to each other. In the poem, that is what connects the reaper to the persona, and both to us as readers. And that is what always connects us to the world and to each other. The richness of the persona's mindful process, attentive to a full range of perceptual relationships, reverberates for us as readers through time, space, and human memory.³

Between its beginning and its ending, the poem engages the concrete beauty of one particular person "beholding" one particular woman singing one particular song in one particular field. And simultaneously it engages the reader in a similar moment of beautiful experience *and* models the way of entering into such beautiful experiences at any point in time and space. It both enters into and propagates the dance of perception, the play of mindfulness in the world, beginning with the woman's rhythmic reaping and singing, beginning again with the persona's witnessing and altered state of mind, and providing the reader with yet another point of beginning in his or her own experience of the poem. The poem as a whole is not simply an artifact to be "examined" or "appreciated," but a moment of perception to be participated in—a point of entry into a process of knowing.

Some Conclusions and New Directions

"The Solitary Reaper" celebrates the connections that we all share—of meaning-making, creative process, and partial knowledge—and provides a good example with which to conclude this discussion of Wordsworth's rhetorical epistemology. For over a hundred years, critics have tended to dismiss or undervalue Wordsworth's "philosophy," following Matthew Arnold's lead. Arnold correctly claimed that Wordsworth's poetry was worst when he attempted to be systematic, didactic, and philosophic. But Arnold assumed, in typical Victorian style, that this philosophical failure removed Wordsworth from the field of significant knowledge-seeking. Arnold's critique had the inevitable effect of encouraging readers to see Wordsworth's poetry as an escape from a "real life" that was becoming more and more ugly, impersonal, and unmanageable.

Arnold's reading is typical of Victorian "high seriousness," and it represents the central belief of our time that knowledge and pleasure are two completely different and irreconcilable pursuits. On one hand, we have the categories of work, information, progress, and knowledge; on the other hand, we have play, pleasure, fantasy, and recreation. By wedding two forms of Puritanism—religious and scientific—Western culture has created a model of knowledge that is both amazingly effective and terrifyingly inhuman. In that model, knowledge is a *product* of intellect and reason. Knowledge is seen as a quantity of information abstracted or generalized from sensual experience and stored by the mind, which is separate from, and in an adversarial relationship with, the body. The mind is further broken down into 'cognitive' and 'emotive' functions—one of which stores and uses knowledge, the other of which simply reacts or responds irrationally to the force of circumstances. True knowledge, according to the puritanisms we have cultivated, must be free from emotional influences, physical desires, and any other subjective elements. Indeed, true knowledge must be freed from all the contexts of daily life, so that it can be applied universally without regard to such contexts. We see equations—"$E=mc^2$" and "$F=ma$"—as the epitome of knowledge, because they are linear, objective, and exact. They seem to be free from the "taint" of affective and subjective complexities; they offer us a knowledge that we can rely on because it is not subject to the negotiations, remediations, and circumstantial reconsiderations that we deal with so much in our everyday lives.

But such "objective" knowledge is of little or no worth when it is not applied and reshaped within the field of human value judgments. As human beings, we must continually determine courses of action within a complicated web of human and natural motives, desires, and relations. We know, as living, breathing individuals, that very few, if any, of our daily decisions are shaped by scientific or systematic knowledge. We don't concern ourselves with the momentum of falling apples or the atomic structure of desks on a daily basis as we work, as we make choices about getting along with family and friends, caring for our children, eating and sleeping and making love. As Kenneth Burke asserts, "acts are not 'true' and 'false' in the sense that the propositions of 'scientific realism' are" (44). Most decisions are moral decisions. What is the right thing to do? And what is the best way to do it? These questions are much more important to us in our daily lives than any of the questions that science attempts to answer.

For Wordsworth, knowledge always begins in, and is sustained by, moments like the one in which the persona sees and hears the solitary reaper in the field. It is first and foremost a function of relationship—of listening and valuing—rather than of fact-gathering. This is what

Wordsworth meant when he wrote that poetry is the "breath and finer spirit of all knowledge": poetry is the process by which logos challenges itself. To know always requires an extension of one's self and one's views into the unknown, and that act always threatens (and promises) change. Creativity and morality are both functions of this extension of the self into the unknown through engaging the kairos. Only by letting go of the self can we renew the self; only by letting go of our prejudices can we act morally toward those who are "borderers," only by letting go of our narrow views can we see and feel what others see and feel. Imagination, rather than reason, is the process that allows for logos to be both constructed and deconstructed. And it is the force that connects beauty, conduct, and truth, all of which are functions of right relationship in kairos.

Wordsworth sensed that scientific epistemology, which was rapidly "proving" itself (in a self-fulfilling prophecy), was inadequate because it left out entire dimensions of human knowing. The personal was being devalued by "objectivity," the beautiful was being devalued by "realism," the creative was being devalued by the "useful and efficient," and the moral (which deals in recognizing potential problems, avoiding problems by choosing right courses of action, and alleviating insoluble problems) was being devalued by a focus on instrumental reason and solutions. Wordsworth did not disdain science at all, but he felt that science was not enough. What he did was to position poetry as a process of mind that could complete science.

Poetry, for Wordsworth, is the ongoing process of returning to perception and remaking meaning; it is the self-revision of logos in kairos. Poetry connects and brings to life both "objective knowledge" and "personal experience" by showing that both emerge from each other and both are valuable. "The Solitary Reaper," like most of Wordsworth's best compositions, does not represent a moment's escape from real, factual, working, knowledge-seeking and knowledge-employing experience. Instead, it represents the first work of knowing and attempting to share knowledge. Wordsworth's compositions invite us to participate in moments of experience and to make something of value from them—to use them as we compose our view of ourselves and our place in the web of relationships that make up our world. They offer us a different model of knowledge founded on relationship, negotiation, and composition itself.

Postscript
Using Wordsworth's Model of Knowing

> [The dance of the honeybees] is probably not to be understood as producing in the 'minds' of the bees a form of knowledge in reflective correspondence with the flowers. Rather, it is an activity, which, when properly carried out, acts as a pointer or indicator, disposing the bees to an order of action that will generally lead them to the honey.
> —David Bohm, *Wholeness and the Implicate Order*

> Comprehension of the totality [of all that is] is not a reflective correspondence between 'thought' and 'reality as a whole.' Rather it is to be considered as an art form, like poetry, which may dispose us toward order and harmony in the overall 'dance of the mind' (and thus in the general functioning of the brain and nervous system).
> —David Bohm, *Wholeness and the Implicate Order*

> by obeying ... the impulses of those habits, we shall describe objects, and utter sentiments, of such a nature, and in such connection with each other, that the understanding of the Reader must necessarily be in some degree enlightened, and his affections strengthened and purified.
> —William Wordsworth, 1802 Preface to *Lyrical Ballads*

In the first pages of this book, I wrote that this text "should be considered as an experiment in critical discourse—an attempt both to discuss and embody an alternative model of knowing." Now it is time to explain how and why this is so ... and why it matters. My experiment in this text was to attempt to show the development of a line of thinking in praxis: not to set forth a model at the beginning, and then to apply it in the rest of the text, but to show the explorations and inquiries that led to a model, and then gradually to articulate it. I aimed to take a transdisciplinary approach which did not subordinate one discourse to another, which avoided easy oppositions and highlighted boundary complications rather than trying to resolve them. As a result, the text aims to combine theory and application into *praxis*, and to embody the natural connections of literary study, rhetoric, and systems theory. It has been constructed to highlight the relationships between multiple levels of context for analysis, and between multiple disciplinary approaches, rather than to isolate a problem from context or to deal with it as if only one context mattered. It has been constructed to highlight questions, rather than to answer them. It seeks to open and sustain inquiry rather than to close it.

In that spirit, I will conclude this exploration, and hopefully open further explorations, by claiming here that (1) our most pressing challenge in higher education today is to find a satisfactory replacement for the reason-centered, Cartesian model of knowing, (2) the best alternative models available are ones which center, like Wordsworth's, on developing and sustaining an ecology of mind, and (3) the "disciplines" best-equipped for meeting this challenge are rhetoric, systems science, and literary study—and the three are fundamentally related and well-suited for collaborative inquiry.

I

Matthew Arnold, although he helped found many misunderstandings about Wordsworth, sounds very like Wordsworth when he reminds us in "Literature and Science"(1882) that science (and, by implication, instrumental reason) is not adequate to the broader mission of education. In his response to Thomas Henry Huxley, he claims that although the advances in knowledge being offered by scientists were great,

> still it will be *knowledge* only which they give us; knowledge not put into relation with our sense for conduct, our sense for beauty, and touched with emotion by being so put; not thus put for us, and therefore, to the majority of mankind, after a certain while, unsatisfying, wearying. (390)

Arnold argued that education could not depend on science alone, because science limited itself to the advancement of technical knowledge. What Arnold longed for, and felt to be slipping out of his culture's grasp, was the unity of what the Greeks called *aretê*. What he feared, and did not go so far as to say in this particular case, was that "unsatisfying" and "wearying" were not strong enough terms for knowledge that was separated from "the sense for beauty, the sense for conduct."

In the final years of the twentieth century, as we face the long-term results of the scientific model of knowledge, we must acknowledge the foresight of both Wordsworth and Arnold on this issue. A generation ago, E. F. Schumacher—one of the most humane economic theorists of this century—criticized the implicit superiority of scientific knowledge, and of education leading to such knowledge, in C. P. Snow's argument about the "two cultures." He believed that ideas about education which attempt to bridge the gap between scientific and humanistic knowledge by making sure that everyone has adequate *scientific* knowledge are poor ideas indeed:

> These ideas on education, which are by no means unrepresentative of our times, leave one with the uncomfortable feeling that ordinary people, including politicians, administrators, and so forth, are really not much use; they have failed to make the grade: but, at least, they should be educated enough to have a sense of what is going on, and to know what the scientists mean when they talk—to quote Lord Snow's example—about the Second Law of Thermodynamics. It is an uncomfortable feeling, because the scientists never tire of telling us that the fruits of their labours are "neutral": whether they enrich humanity or destroy it depends on how they are used. And who is to decide how they are used? There is nothing in the training of scientists and engineers to enable them to take such decisions, or else, what becomes of the neutrality of science? (81)

Scientific positivism, by claiming objectivity and value neutrality even as it claims absolute authority in the discovery of knowledge, places us in the uncomfortable position of having vast reserves of explanation and technique and "verifiable fact" without any way of valuing, or applying valuably, all that explanation and technique and "verifiable fact." Knowledge that is unscientific is treated as non-knowledge, yet since science claims no moral position, all moral knowledge must be seen as mere opinion—unverifiable and subjective.

And that is why science and specialized knowledge—what Wordsworth called "Reason sequester'd" in *The Prelude*—can be so very dangerous. They are removed from, and provide no direction or value for, the individual acting in the world. As Kenneth Burke asserts:

> If the technical expert, as such, is assigned the task of perfecting new powers of chemical, bacteriological, or atomic destruction, his morality as technical expert requires only that he apply himself to his task as effectively as possible. The question of what the new force might mean, as released into a social texture emotionally and intellectually unfit to control it, or as surrendered to men whose

specialty is professional killing—well, that is simply "none of his business," as specialist, however great may be his misgivings as father of a family, or as citizen of his nation and the world. (30)

Our postmodern world is filled with the terrifying results of technical knowledge misapplied, of scientific "advances" which have proven to be moral disasters. As Berman states, the broad adoption of scientific epistemology has placed us on the brink of extinction.

Rhetoric and systems theory—two of the critical frameworks applied in this text—provide a better understanding of why this is so. A colleague who read this book in draft form stated that he could not believe that I would seriously assert that "bad thinking" or a bad "model of knowing" could be equivalent to "evil." But I am asserting just that. Rhetoricians, ecologists, and other systems thinkers have all shown that the failure to recognize and relate to others (other people, other viewpoints, other systems, other creatures) leads to disaster. As I see it, the failure to relate with others is one face of evil. This face of evil appears whenever a person treats another person with hatred because they have reduced that other person to a particular category ("poor" or "dumb" or "black" or even "cop," for instance). It appears whenever we treat persons or creatures as objects to use and utilize, rather than as other minds to relate with. It is the form of evil that Martin Buber explores in *I and Thou*.

This face of evil also appears on a larger scale when one person, one community, or one nation attempts to claim knowledge as a possession to be held and exercised over others and on others (even for "their own good") rather than recognizing the knowledge of others and entering into the rhetorical processes of knowing them better.

I believe that Wordsworth's thinking and poetry emerged from his desire to combat such evil. He felt that a mode of knowing in which beauty, conduct, and knowledge were not united and interrelated was bound to be destructive, and he sought to found a different approach that would bring healing to his culture. Not the healing of escapism, as Arnold seemed to say in "Memorial Verses," his elegy for Wordsworth, but the healing of listening, reflecting, and learning. Wordsworth believed that if we participate completely in our relationships with ourselves, with others, and with the world, our sensibilities will be broadened and our moral position necessarily improved.

As an experienced teacher, I cannot be as optimistic about the idea that simply sharing experiences will bring "relationship and love." But I think that if we accept that we only have operative knowledge within the limited domain of our own experience, we might not treat people or animals or the world as things to be manipulated. If we accept—as the Sophists did—that no system of values is ever "absolute" but only a set of more or less useful guidelines, and if we accept—as systems thinkers are beginning to do—that our "selves" are not autonomous beings who can use the world as we see fit (but rather shifting and growing parts of a whole process of relation involving our environment, our relationships with others, and our ideas), then we have no impetus to commit atrocities on others or to create social orders that impoverish the individuals who participate in them. The social order should not be seen as a "contract" but as an ongoing set of relations, which must be fluid and continually re-negotiated. This is why democracy has flourished as a form of government, despite its weaknesses—it comes closer than other existing forms of government to acknowledging the natural form of human relations. As Kenneth Burke asserts, we are all individuals in search of unity with others, in search of membership in larger processes which give us meaning and value as individuals. In many ways, it is the failure of relational rhetoric, and the lack of broader awareness of our place within larger living systems, that lead to binary oppositions and destruction and evil.

Unfortunately, relational rhetoric is neither acknowledged nor taught in a rational model of knowing. And as Gregory Bateson convincingly argues,

> mere purposive rationality unaided by such phenomena as art, religion, dream, and the like, is necessarily pathogenic and destructive of life; ... its virulence springs specifically from the circumstance that life depends upon interlocking circuits of contingency, while consciousness can see only such short arcs of such circuits as human purpose may direct. (Bateson, *Steps to an Ecology of Mind* 146)

Systems of thought tend to map the "circuits" of living systems clearly and finally, and then encourage the development of rational purposes as if those circuits were known in their entirety. We tend to represent the circuits of life as best we can, and then to accept our representations as real. From then on, we manipulate experience rather than being receptive to re-vising it. And that is a major epistemological mistake.

II

To remedy that epistemological mistake, we need a better model of knowing. To envision that model and put it to work, the machine-centered metaphors of Newton and Descartes must be replaced. But by what? Critics of Romanticism such as M. H. Abrams have suggested that Romantic thinkers attempted to replace machine metaphors with organic metaphors. But he, like most critics, assumes the single plant as the core of organic metaphors. And he recognizes, to some extent, the manifold shortcomings of such a metaphor. In the single-plant organic model, the seed contains everything that the plant will become. Associated characteristics emerge gradually and insensibly rather than being the result of clearly-defined mechanical causes, but those characteristics are part of the plant from the very start. The plant uses its environment as material for self-creation, but that environment does not fundamentally change it.

This model is far too simple to contain Wordsworth's complex vision of mental process. In this text, I have suggested that his interest in the larger processes of nature encouraged him to elaborate a model of knowing that can best be conceived of as *environmental* or *ecological*. Rather than focusing on the machine metaphor so predominant in his time, or the one-dimensional organic metaphor espoused by Coleridge, he chose an approach which accepted the necessity of diversity, which took for granted the many complex interchanges between minds and between mind and world, and which centered on the complications of relationship and boundary issues rather than attempting to resolve them.

In this text I have identified his model as an "ecology of mind," connecting it to the model developed in Bateson's work. The central metaphor employed in these models is an ecosystem that encompasses physical and mental processes at multiple, interrelated levels. In this model, adaptive learning and evolution are the moving principles. And all learning or evolving depends on engagement with others. Different people contribute different views, and the well-being of the culture depends on the diversity and engagement of the individuals that constitute it.

Within such an ecosystem, identity and value are functions of relationship. A living system can only place itself, and place a value on itself, in reference to other living systems. Wordsworth also intuitively recognized this, and believed that the only way to attain moral understanding was to challenge and re-negotiate our own logos—our "pre-established codes of decision"—by participating in "larger processes." We have a responsibility to listen to the voices of others, to attempt to identify with their situation, and to respond to (and, when necessary, to attempt to redefine) the larger social and natural processes in which we play a role.

In an ecology of mind, meaning and value are always composed, mediated by personal experience, and context-bound. In short, meaning and value are always matters of interpretation. But that does not make them "subjective" in the condescending sense used by logical positivists. Instead, it places them in the field of knowing. "Objectivity" is a stance taken towards experience, and there is no way to make the logos look exactly like the flux of life that we cannot talk about without language. Interpretation and meaning production are central concerns of the poet and the literary scholar. And they are also central concerns of the rhetorician and the systems scientist. This is the core that binds these different disciplines together. We compose our experience, and we are composed by our experience. We carry on an endless dialogue with what we have been, what we are, and what we hope to be. And that dialogue is not only with ourselves, but with our families, our neighbors, our co-workers, and with the broader logos of our society.

The process of interacting with others is transactional, and we must be aware of multiple levels of context in order to learn or evolve successfully. If we cannot get outside of our own logos, we are trapped absolutely. Only imagination and participation in larger systems can free us. Imagination which is unrestrained and undisciplined simply leads us into visionary worlds of our own making. But imagination which is receptive to experience, and to others' experience, and which is trained by disciplined engagement, allows us to develop self-correcting habits of mind that are sound.

III

Rhetoric, systems theory, and literary study—the critical discourses that I have engaged in this text—can be fruitfully related and collaboratively employed to develop inquiry into the ecology of mind.

The process of developing a complex, recursive, evolutionary view of mindful patterns and activities in the living world is already underway in the sciences. The disciplines of literary study and rhetoric are well equipped to join and further this effort. Systems theory, chaos theory, and other scientific advances can provide literary study and rhetoric with conceptual models that help articulate the complexities of texts and their many contexts.

Rhetoric, as it has been interpreted and applied in this text, is the symbolic construction of meaning. It is a transactional process that consists of the engagement of particular contexts (kairos) within the broader system of meaning established by logos. In Wordsworth's model of knowing, "Poetry" and "Science" would be considered two forms of discourse on a rhetorical spectrum rather than two separate areas of activity. At one end of the spectrum, we have positivistic science, which operates within the logos, the existing structures of symbolic meaning, and makes every attempt to firm up the logos—to finalize meaning. At the other end, we have the poetry of imaginative vision, which challenges (and refuses) the logos by creating visionary worlds. Moving toward the center of the spectrum, we reach the points at which creative thinking and objective analysis or study meet—where reflection and feeling, vision and reality, beauty and truth, become interrelated. This is the place where rhetoric is most effective, and where change is wrought. And according to Wordsworth, it is accessible to all of us.

The effective rhetor always attempts to establish a position near the center of the spectrum. In order to engage human experience effectively, scientists must overcome the temptation of totalizing abstractions and mechanistic oversimplifications in order to acknowledge complexity (as those working in quantum physics, chaos theory, cybernetics, neuroscience, and other fields now recognize). Similarly, poets must overcome the temptation to drift in worlds of completely personal visionary experience in order to engage perception—their own and their audience's. Wordsworth understood this need. He placed poetry in the role of a natural and necessary complement to science, and worked with the empirical commitment of science. His poetry appeals to the logos even as it attempts to shift it or change it. It operates using accepted forms and ideas, while simultaneously deconstructing and reconstructing those forms and ideas. Thus I have argued that his work is always rhetorically-engaged, rather than "expressive."

Rhetoric is always the engagement of multiple systems within an overarching system, and this is why systems theory can provide a helpful "objective" framework for discussing important rhetorical concepts. When two people engage each other, they must find common ground for the engagement. They both are members of an overarching logos, or constructed reality, that provides them with the shared means of talking to one another. Yet simultaneously they are different systems, with different personal logos. Their views are similar enough to share discussion, but different enough to create friction. And this is the point at which learning and meaning-making are possible. It is the friction between similar systems, and between systems and the larger systems in which they play a part, that leads to "differences that make a difference." There is a predominant logos of the times, but each individual carries his or her own idiosyncratic version of it. Shifts in the personal logos of others are possible, and emergent shifts of the overarching logos are a matter of course over time. Wordsworth's insight is that cultural change depends absolutely on personal change. As Quintilian knew, rhetoric always begins with personal commitment to the good. Public good and well-being emerge, in short, not from the "rights" of the individuals, but from the rhetorical engagement (participation, education, and responsibility) of those individuals.

Participation, education, and responsibility. Beauty, knowledge, and conduct. These connections are profound, and profoundly available. All that is required is a shift in emphasis, a shift in the predominant metaphors for understanding the ways we know. In education, our aim should be to pursue and foster valuable lines of inquiry among ourselves and our students. Engagement and connection must be revalidated and exercised as the invaluable counterparts of analysis and examination. In this view, art and literature can be seen (and experienced) as rhetorically-engaged efforts to reshape the logos. Rhetoric and systems theory can provide working concepts to help us articulate the relationships connecting texts, the cultures and ecosystems in which they were produced, and the audiences which they have addressed through history. They provide us with a process-oriented, evolutionary, reconstructive approach to the interpretation of the ecology of mind: a meeting-place for the sciences and the humanities.

Notes

Introduction

1. See Chapter 2 of Bohm's *Wholeness and the Implicate Order*. His contention is that it is hard to talk about the character of interrelationships using a language that reifies objects and consciousnesses. He asserts that we must find a way to talk about states of movement and interaction, and the qualities thereof, more effectively.
2. Since completing this manuscript, I have discovered one study that is dedicated specifically to Wordsworth's epistemology. Terranella's *The Piagetian Epistemology of William Wordsworth* makes the interesting claim that Wordsworth's epistemology can be best understood not in terms of empiricism or idealism, but in terms of a relativism like that of Jean Piaget. Terranella makes interesting connections and offers some general claims about Wordsworth and Romanticism that are helpful (see particularly pages 19–20). But he does not attempt, as I do here, to treat Wordsworth's work as an "epistemic experiment" or to show how Wordsworth uses his alternative epistemology to make claims about the significance of poetry as a substantive discourse of knowledge. He states that we should see "pre-logical" poetry and "logical" science as "parallel modes, each systematically entire and self-sufficient, each shedding light upon the other, each concerned with giving information about the world according to its own genius" (5). Unfortunately, this is another Cartesian divide like those that I discuss later in my introduction.
3. Arnold writes, in his Preface to the 1879 edition of Wordsworth's works, that we must be on our guard against the "Wordsworthians," if we want to secure for Wordsworth his "due rank as a poet. The Wordsworthians are apt to praise him for the wrong things and to lay far too much stress upon what they call his philosophy. His poetry is the reality, his philosophy,—so far, at least, as it may put on the form and habit of a 'scientific system of thought,' and the more that it puts them on,—is the illusion … we cannot do him justice until we dismiss his formal philosophy" (340–41).
4. Jonathan Bate, *Romantic Ecology*; Karl Kroeber, *Ecological Literary Criticism*; Regina Hewitt, *Wordsworth and the Empirical Dilemma* and *The Possibilities of Society*.
5. Barbara Schapiro also attempts to offer a non-Cartesian framework in her article "Wordsworth and the Psychoanalytic Relational Model," but psychoanalysis itself remains entrenched in the view that only humans have "minds." As a result, the relational model she posits includes only social relations, and neglects the relationship between the individual and his or her natural environment—an omission that Wordsworth would have found impossible to tolerate.
6. In his books *Steps to an Ecology of Mind*, *Mind and Nature*, and *Angels Fear*,

Gregory Bateson lays the groundwork for what he calls a "Creatural science" that unites the study of atoms and the study of consciousness in a non-reductive way. He redefines "mind" in broader terms, substitutes Jung's distinction between "pleroma" and "creatura" for Descartes's distinction between "mind" and "matter," and provides a rigorous framework within which to examine evolution, epigenesis, cultural patterns, and human learning as mindful processes—as, in fact, elements in an "ecology of mind." While he has not yet received as much recognition as he deserves, his work embodies the most carefully-considered and potentially useful alternative to the reductive science that has emerged from the Cartesian/Newtonian tradition.

7. Damasio's *Descartes' Error* offers a cogent argument for viewing the workings of "mind" in terms of a continuum of "physical" and "mental" processes of representation.
8. C.C. Clarke's *Romantic Paradox* offers an insightful treatment of Wordsworth's central stress on perception, and his employment of paradox to simulate it. But his analysis focuses on the representation of subjective perceptions and concludes with a recognition that Wordsworth's uses of language represent a "more subtle play of mind than is usually conceded—even by his admirers" (101). And that doesn't do justice to Wordsworth's struggle to generate *and share* a more meaningful view of mind and world.
9. Locke refers repeatedly to "External Objects" as a point of reference; the implicit assumption is that reality exists and our sensations of it are more or less "clear and distinct." See, for example, Book 2, Chapter 1 of the *Essay Concerning Human Understanding*, where Locke claims that all Ideas come from "Experience" and divides experiences into two categories: "Our Observation employ'd either about *external, sensible Objects; or about the internal Operations of our Minds, perceived and reflected on by our selves* ..." (104).
10. "An Essay on Criticism," lines 297–298 (Pope 153).
11. In the "old regime," tradition was the primary source of authority and knowledge. People acted in certain ways because they had been taught to act in those ways—they had been trained to see reality in terms of cultural traditions, customs, and habits. In the "new regime," the primary source of authority was "Reason" and the power of the mind to make sense of the world without regard for the oppressive structures of tradition. People could rely on a higher authority than existing orders and modes of thinking—the authority of their own view of things, guided by the power of reason. So Burke and other thinkers of the time were faced on one hand with oppressive political orders which had no regard for the rights of the individual—and with privileged language structures and modes of representation (crowns, property issues, and so on) that had created and sustained such political orders. But on the other hand lay a new form of tyranny based nominally on "Reason" (and rational discourse), but embodied terrifyingly for Burke in the French Revolution.
12. See Hoopes for an extensive and interesting discussion of "Right Reason" that provides helpful context for considerations of the shifting face of Reason in the eighteenth and nineteenth centuries in England.

Chapter 1

1. For a more complete summary of the fusion of Platonic and Aristotelian principles into Scientific Method, see Chapter 1 of Berman's *Reenchantment of the World*.
2. Parrish, in his *Art of the Lyrical Ballads*, remarks on the rhetorical nature of Wordsworth's poetic theory, but he neglects the epistemological importance of this quote entirely.
3. Aristotle begins *On Rhetoric* with the claim that "Rhetoric is an antistrophos to dialectic; for both are concerned with such things as are, to a certain extent, within the knowledge of all people, and belong to no separately-defined science" ([1345a], 1: 1). He asserts that the two are both types of reasoning, but that dialectic is concerned with "the true" and the demonstrable, while rhetoric is concerned with "what resembles the true" ([1355a], 1: 11) and the probable.
4. In *Wordsworth and the Empirical Dilemma*, Hewitt claims that Wordsworth was interested in developing a relationship with his readers, but that he had to deal with significant changes in the poetry-reading "audience" of his times. As a result, he attempted to find many ways to involve his readers in what he was doing, and his work appears inconsistent in form and approach as a result of a coherent process of experimentation.
5. For a brief and intelligent discussion of Gorgias' arguments and their interpretations in later literature, see Kerferd's *The Sophistic Movement*, pages 93–99.
6. For a summary of Protagoras' doctrine and its philosophical implications and reception, see Kerferd, pages 85–93. Also see Untersteiner's variant translation of the doctrine on page 42ff in *The Sophists*. He claims that a more accurate translation is: "Man is the master of experiences," and takes a different approach to the doctrine accordingly. But in either case, the philosophical problem of beginning with personal experience and accepting contradictions among the experiences had by different people, remains central. Is such contradiction a problem to be "resolved" as Plato and Descartes and a host of others try to resolve it? Or is it a condition of life to be explored and put to use in our language and thought and law? Wordsworth's paradoxes and stress on individual perception are evidence that he chose the second path.
7. John Nabholtz ("Classical Rhetoric") provides, in a succinct article, a helpful reminder of the central role that classical rhetoric played in the education of romantic writers and the influence that it had on "romantic prose." The influence that classical rhetoric may have had on the *poetry* of these authors is only now beginning to be investigated.

Chapter 2

1. Postman argues that our technologies, particularly communication technologies, implicitly make some of our decisions about what knowledge is. He offers a nice discussion of "Media as Epistemology" in his penetrating book *Amusing Ourselves to Death: Public Discourse in the Age of Show Business*, illustrating some of the

ways in which sources of authority were undermined and reconstructed as we moved from oral to written to electronic modes of expression. I extend his position here to include the shift from narrative-centered writing mode into expository writing mode.

2. This interpretation came from physicists' painful grappling with experimental facts. In essence, it asserted that we have no way of establishing a one-to-one correspondence between our theories and some "absolute truth" that exists "out there." We cannot know the details of every individual subatomic event because they are shrouded in a mystery that emerges from the very structure of reality. What we CAN do is predict with great certainty the probabilities of particular behaviors of aggregates of matter and energy. For helpful accounts of this interpretation and its implications for modern science, see books such as Bohm's *Wholeness and the Implicate Order* and Zukav's *The Dancing Wu Li Masters*.

3. Rader, Grob, Durrant, and many others have pursued and attempted to establish clearly just what Wordsworth's philosophical position(s) was/were. I am not questioning the details of their accounts of his philosophy here, but simply stressing the fact that a central thread in the vast fabric of Wordsworth scholarship has been preoccupied with the issue.

4. Many critics have made this assumption. A good example is provided by Hayden in *Polestar of the Ancients*. He considers Wordsworth's and Coleridge's ideas about "creative theory" to be essentially the same, and goes so far as to claim that "Coleridge was probably the source of many of his [Wordsworth's] ideas about literary creativity" (183). He also claims that Wordsworth "tends toward a mixture of incompatible epistemologies, the empiricist and the transcendental—'Hartley transcendentalized by Coleridge' in Ernest de Selincourt's formula" (183). Clearly, de Selincourt takes the same view: that Wordsworth's ideas owe much, if not everything, to Coleridge.

5. Coleridge often places himself in the role of thinker and Wordsworth in the role of "poet." One good example of this appropriation occurs in the Chapter 4 of the *Biographia Literaria*, where Coleridge writes that: "it was Mr. Wordsworth's purpose to consider the influences of fancy and imagination as they are manifested in poetry, and from the different effects to conclude their diversity in kind; while it is my object to investigate the seminal principle, and then from the kind to deduce the degree. My friend has drawn a masterly sketch of the branches with their *poetic* fruitage. I wish to add the trunk, and even the roots, as far as they lift themselves above ground and are visible to the naked eye of our common consciousness" (52). Here Coleridge clearly offers a nod at Wordsworth's poetic ability but claims for himself the role of profound, systematic thinker—of the philosopher explaining the structure of the mind. Chandler's final chapter, "The Role of Coleridge" (235–65), provides a nice discussion of the divergence between the two authors along these lines.

6. Bialostosky, "Coleridge's Interpretation of Wordsworth's Preface to *Lyrical Ballads*," *PMLA* 93 (October 1978): 912–24.

7. In the *Gorgias*, the *Phaedrus*, and many other dialogues, Plato makes it clear that he dismisses sophistry and eristic as idle contention, as opposed to the earnest search

for Truth that he claims for dialectic. But as Kerferd notes, it "has been well said that the word 'dialectic' had a strong tendency in Plato to mean 'the ideal method, *whatever* that may be'" (65). And by the same token, substituting the Forms for "reality" enabled Plato to use language to discuss a truth that could not be tested by direct experience. This use of language for personal ends is the essence of what Plato himself dismisses as "sophistry."

8. See Marrou and Kimball for informative discussions of this shift from Isocratean to Platonic assumptions in education.
9. Sebberson makes the very valuable claim that Wordsworth was more interested in pragmatic thinking and reasoning, rather than in abstract philosophy. He ties Wordsworth to the rhetorical tradition, but does not address Wordsworth's epistemology.

Chapter 3

1. Damasio and Bateson both point out the problem of relying on what Descartes called a "homunculus" (or a self within the self) in order to explain perception. The soul is in the pineal gland, according to Descartes, and that provides no way to get from the *matter* of "extension" to the *mind* of self (without an endless regress of perceiving minds within bodies).
2. In this text, passages from the *Prelude* are quoted from *The Prelude 1799, 1805, 1850* (Wordsworth, Abrams, and Gill). Each passage will include a citation which indicates the version (1799, 1805, 1850) of *The Prelude* and the appropriate book and line numbers. For example: 1805 *Prelude* 10: 288–300.
3. The quote comes from John Locke, who makes this distinction about the exercise of reason in his *Essay Concerning Human Understanding*, Book 2, Chapter 11, Section 13: "*mad Men* ... do not appear to me to have lost the Faculty of Reasoning: but having joined together some *Ideas* very wrongly, they mistake them for Truths; and they err as Men do, that argue right from wrong Principles. For by the violence of their Imaginations, having taken their Fancies for Realities, they make right deductions from them" (161).
4. Stoddard suggests this in her consideration of *The Borderers*. She claims that "instead of merely showing how dangerous reason can be in making moral judgments, the play tends to discredit the power of reason to motivate action at all" (96). This point holds true for much of Wordsworth's poetry as well. He most often implies that action is impelled by feeling or "pleasure" (Preface to *Lyrical Ballads*), by engagement with the world, rather than by reflective reasoning.
5. According to his letters, Wordsworth read Erasmus Darwin's *Zoonomia* with great interest. In a letter to Joseph Cottle (his publisher) dated Feb 28 (or Mar 7), 1798, he requests a copy of the text post haste. In a letter dated May 9, 1798, he sends it back to Cottle with comments indicating that he has read it eagerly (*LWDW* 218). More inquiry into his connection of biology, "ecosystems," and thinking follows in later chapters of this text.

Chapter 4

1. It is significant that Wordsworth puts himself in the position of combating evil here; in the context in which this passage occurs, Wordsworth clearly sees as evil the conditions of his culture that are acting to "blunt the discriminating powers of the mind" and to create a "degrading thirst after outrageous stimulation." And at the core of that evil is a failure of perception and of the relational rhetoric that relies on good perception. I return to this point in my postscript.
2. The quote comes from a letter to John Wilson dated [Jun 7, 1802], in which Wordsworth stresses the issue of reader participation greatly. He responds to Wilson's earlier letter praising the *Lyrical Ballads*, writing that "It is plain from your letter that the pleasure which I have given you has not been blind or unthinking you have studied the poems and prove that you have entered into the spirit of them" (*LWDW* 353).

Chapter 5

1. The idea of a pre-existing reality is apparent, for example, in Locke's distinction between primary and secondary qualities—the prior inheres in the things themselves and the latter in the mind of the perceiver. The difficulty, of course, is determining which qualities of "things" are truly "primary" and which are "secondary." How can we examine the validity of our assumptions about "primary" qualities when we have no access to "things themselves" and are limited to direct perception of our own "Ideas"?
2. The most famous examples, of course, are Descartes, who had to assume a "beneficent God" in order to assure that he wasn't being tricked by false sense data, and Berkeley, who avoided solipsism by positing a world of mentality in which individuals were ideas in the mind of God.
3. Jonathan Bate, in *Romantic Ecology* (1991), argues for a reading of Wordsworth which recognizes the centrality of his ecological vision. Bate makes many valuable points about the political significance of Wordsworth's ecological principles. He shows how readings that attempt to place Wordsworth in one political camp or the other ("Left" or "Right") miss an entire dimension of Wordsworth's thinking. For him, "An 'ideology' based on a harmonious relationship with nature goes beyond, in many ways goes deeper than, the political model we have become used to thinking with" (19). Interestingly enough, he also connects Wordsworth's project to Gregory Bateson's. I think that Bate's book and this study consider facets of the same central problem in Wordsworth criticism. My goal here is to connect Wordsworth's "ecology" both to the tradition of rhetoric and to the broader view of ecology that Bateson began developing in *Steps to an Ecology of Mind*.

Chapter 6

1. Bateson originally sets forth these terms in *Mind and Nature*; a succinct discussion of his ideas is included on pages 20–21 of *Angels Fear*. In essence, he claims that "The map is not the territory. The name is not the thing named" (*Angels Fear* 21). From this basic understanding he builds up a view of mental process which centers on symbolic negotiation of "difference"—yet which cannot be reduced to symbolic logic. Throughout his discussion, he shows that the essence of mind is not simply the PROCESSING of information, but the ORGANIZING of information into patterns of value and meaning that lead to action. Here he and Wordsworth would have agreed completely.
2. Abrams wrote the rest of this passage off as half-baked associationism, and many others have followed suit.
3. This example of emergence was drawn from a web site dedicated to systems thinking. See *http://www.radix.net/~crbnblu/systems/emergence.htm* for the example.
4. This point is supported by many recent advances in science, the discussion of which is necessarily beyond the scope of this book. Of particular interest, however, is the exploration of self-organizing systems being carried on by scientists like Nobel laureate Ilya Prigogine. His book *Order Out of Chaos: Man's New Dialogue with Nature* (1984) offers transformative insights into the way that "order" can emerge from apparent randomness.

Chapter 7

1. See David Sebberson's article, which associates Wordsworth with rhetoric within its history as "practical reasoning," and states that "approaching rhetoric as a means of practical reasoning rather than as a series of (purely) linguistic devices allows for a critique of the manner in which the ethical and the political are articulated. As such, rhetoric is not concerned so much with linguistic play as with *human action and the language that governs it* [my emphasis]" (97).
2. I do not have the time or space to examine this question fully here, but the question is well worth asking.
3. Wordsworth scholarship has only recently begun to steer away from the powerful, but often misleading, generalizations about English Romanticism put forth by M. H. Abrams in *The Mirror and the Lamp*. Several critics have begun to reconsider Wordsworth's rhetorical purposes and methods, or at least to acknowledge that he had such purposes and methods (Altieri "Poetics of Eloquence" and "Preface as Literary Theory," Breyer, Ruoff); their work contradicts Abrams' vision of Wordsworth as the first poet of a movement which focused completely on personal expression and refused to admit rhetorical purpose into the realm of poetic creation and aesthetic pleasure. Other critics have investigated Wordsworth's debts to and connections with classical literary sources and theories (Hayden, Worthington); their work suggests that Abrams was guilty of oversimplification when he claimed

that Wordsworth substituted an "amalgam" of "eighteenth-century speculations" and "prevalent ideas" for "neo-classic theories which had been based more substantially on Aristotle, Horace, Cicero, and Quintilian" (104). Nabholtz ("Classical Rhetoric") connects the two areas of critical inquiry in an article which reminds us of the influence of classical rhetoric on the Romantic poets at large, but he dedicates much of his discussion to a consideration of Coleridge's debt to Cicero. These helpful studies suggest that a closer examination of Wordsworth's use of classical rhetorical sources might lead us to a better understanding of his poetic aims and practices.

4. The Institutes, in turn, show strong connections with Isocrates' ideas. Like Isocrates, Quintilian stresses natural talent and practice over formal training; focuses on the power of language to compose/construct meaning; and constructs public value and meaning on personal responsibility, education, and action. They are both much more concerned with educational processes than with knowledge as an 'end product.'

5. In his book *'My Reader, My Fellow Laborer': A Study of English Romantic Prose*, Nabholtz takes a closer look at Wordsworth's rhetorical ideas and methods, advancing the idea that the goal of Wordsworth's 'Preface' to *Lyrical Ballads* "is *the creation of a mutually understanding and beneficial relationship between reader and writer*," that "Instead of constituting a 'systematic defence' whose purpose would be the demonstrable truth of the propositions advanced, the 'introductory remarks' are rhetorical and apologetic, seeking at best probability or 'presumption' about the truth of the propositions" (Nabholtz, *My Reader* 71). Nabholtz claims that the first five paragraphs of the Preface act as an Exordium, following classical tradition, and that "in the 'Preface,' Wordsworth *as writer* was primarily concerned with *creating a favorably disposed and activated reader*; the success or the failure of the 'Preface' as prose document must be considered in these terms" (80).

    By initiating such a rhetorical discussion of Wordsworth, he moves the scholarly stress away from "inconsistent theory" (cited by Abrams and so many others) and reminds us that Wordsworth was attempting to do something besides establishing a monolithic system of poetry or thought. As authors such as Bialostosky and Breyer have recently pointed out, it is a critical mistake to view Wordsworth's ideas and contributions to literature through the lens of Coleridge's theories. Nabholtz does not, however, apply the rhetorical ideas he discusses to Wordsworth's poetic efforts. This task remains for other critics to pursue.

6. See I. A. Richards' *Philosophy of Rhetoric* for a clear example of this division being used as a critical assumption.

7. In his ground-breaking book *Descartes' Error*, Damasio connects emotion and practical reasoning in a scientific, objective way that lends force to the intuitive and theoretical connections made by Quintilian and Wordsworth himself. He asserts that upper level reasoning processes are grounded in feeling response, and that biological and symbolic representation are the basis of intelligence. Damasio makes connections that Wordsworth also attempted to make: between perception, feeling, and thinking; between images, representations, and meaning-making; and between

mental processes and the physical processes from which they emerge.
8. "Power" is a term that preoccupied Wordsworth, and that remains largely misunderstood because it is considered to be "separate" from knowledge. De Quincey made a distinction between the literature of knowledge and the literature of power which is often attributed to Wordsworth himself, but it is more likely that Wordsworth would place knowledge and power *together* in many significant ways.
9. See Breyer for an interesting comparison of the conceptions of pleasure offered by Wordsworth and Coleridge.

Chapter 8

1. The division between expressive and persuasive uses of language is clearly drawn, for example, in Abrams' "Introduction: Orientation of Critical Theories" (3–29) and Kinneavy's discussion of the "communication triangle" (pages 17–40).
2. See Altieri for a nice discussion of "Wordsworth and the Poetics of Eloquence" which suggests that such transformation is Wordsworth's aim. But Altieri does not deal fully with the complexity of Wordsworth's discursive effort: to generate reader participation which allows for transformative OR incremental learning, and to extend the field of meaning-making beyond single "eloquent" poems and into the reader's engagement with the body of his writing as a whole.
3. I am indebted to Linda Hanson, my dissertation advisor, for this well-wrought sentence. I read it in her notes on a draft, and decided that I could not say it any better.

Works Cited

Abrams, M. H. *The Mirror and the Lamp*. New York: Oxford UP, 1953.
Altieri, Charles. "Wordsworth's Poetics of Eloquence: A Challenge to Contemporary Theory." *Romantic Revolutions: Criticism and Theory*. Ed. Kenneth R. Johnston et al. Bloomington, IN: Indiana UP, 1990. 371–407.
———. "Wordsworth's 'Preface' as Literary Theory." *Criticism* 18 (1976): 122–46.
Aristotle. *On Rhetoric*. Trans. George A. Kennedy. New York: Oxford UP, 1991.
Arnold, Matthew. *Poetry and Criticism of Matthew Arnold*. Ed. A. Dwight Culler. Boston: Houghton Mifflin, 1961.
Bate, Jonathan. *Romantic Ecology: Wordsworth and the Environmental Tradition*. New York: Routledge, 1991.
Bateson, Gregory. *Mind and Nature: A Necessary Unity*. New York: E. P. Dutton, 1979.
———. *Steps to an Ecology of Mind: Collected Essays in Anthropology, Psychiatry, Evolution, and Epistemology*. Northvale, NJ: Jason Aronson, 1972.
Bateson, Gregory, and Mary Catherine Bateson. *Angels Fear: Towards an Epistemology of the Sacred*. New York: Bantam, 1987.
Belenky, Mary Field, Blythe McVicker Clinchy, Nancy Rule Goldberger, and Jill Mattuck Tarule. *Women's Ways of Knowing: The Development of Self, Voice, and Mind*. New York: Basic Books, 1986.
Berman, Morris. *The Reenchantment of the World*. Ithaca, NY: Cornell UP, 1981.
Bialostosky, Don H. "Coleridge's interpretation of Wordsworth's Preface to *Lyrical Ballads*," *PMLA* 93 (1978): 912–24.
———. *Making Tales: the Poetics of Wordsworth's Narrative Experiments*. Chicago: U of Chicago P, 1984.
Bohm, David. *Wholeness and the Implicate Order*. Boston: Routledge & Kegan Paul, 1981.
Breyer, B. R. "Wordsworth's Pleasure: An Approach to his Poetic Theory." *Southern Humanities Review* 6 (1972): 123–31.

Burke, Edmund. *Reflections on the Revolution in France.* New York: Penguin, 1969.
Burke, Kenneth. *A Rhetoric of Motives.* Berkeley, CA: U of California P, 1950.
Bush, Douglas. "Wordsworth: A Minority Report." *Wordsworth: Centenary Studies.* Ed. Gilbert T. Dunklin. Princeton, NJ: Princeton UP, 1951.
Castaneda, Carlos. *Journey to Ixtlan.* New York: Simon and Schuster, 1972.
Chandler, James K. *Wordsworth's Second Nature: A Study of the Poetry and the Politics.* Chicago: U of Chicago P, 1984.
Clarke, C. C. *Romantic Paradox.* New York: Barnes and Noble, 1963.
Danford, John W. *Hume and the Problem of Reason: Recovering the Human Sciences.* New Haven: Yale UP, 1990.
Damasio, Antonio. *Descartes' Error: Emotion, Reason, and the Human Brain.* New York: Putnam, 1994.
Darling, David. *Equations of Eternity: Speculations on Consciousness, Meaning, and the Mathematical Rules that Orchestrate the Cosmos.* New York: Hyperion, 1993.
Descartes, René. *Philosophical Writings.* Indianapolis, IN: Bobbs-Merrill, 1971.
Durrant, Geoffrey. *Wordsworth and the Great System: A Study of Wordsworth's Poetic Universe.* Cambridge: Cambridge UP, 1970.
Engell, James. *The Creative Imagination.* Cambridge, MA: Harvard UP, 1981.
Frost, Robert. "The Figure a Poem Makes." *Robert Frost: Poetry & Prose.* Eds. Edward Connery Lathem and Lawrance Thompson. New York: Holt, Rinehart & Winston, 1972. 393–96.
Garber, Frederick. *Wordsworth and the Poetry of Encounter.* Urbana, IL: U of Illinois P, 1971.
Grob, Alan. *The Philosophic Mind: A Study of Wordsworth's Poetry and Thought, 1797-1805.* Columbus, OH: Ohio State UP, 1973.
———. "Wordsworth and Godwin: A Reassessment." *Studies in Romanticism* 6.2 (1967): 98–119.
Hairston, Maxine. "The Wind of Change: Thomas Kuhn and the Revolution in the Teaching of Writing." *College Composition and Communication* 3.1 (1982): 76–88.

Hartman, Geoffrey. "Wordsworth, *The Borderers*, and 'Intellectual Murder'." *Journal of English and Germanic Philology* 62.4 (1964): 170–83.
Hayden, John O. *Polestar of the Ancients: The Aristotelian Tradition in Classical and English Literary Theory*. Newark, DE: U of Delaware P, 1979.
Hewitt, Regina. "Faery Lands Fit and Forlorn: Keats and the 'Problem' of Wordsworth's Ego." *Essays in Literature* 14.1 (1987): 65–79.

———. *The Possibilities of Society: Wordsworth, Coleridge, and the Sociological Viewpoint of English Romanticism*. Albany, NY: State U of New York P, 1997.

———. *Wordsworth and the Empirical Dilemma*. New York: Peter Lang, 1990.

Hoopes, Robert. *Right Reason in the English Renaissance*. Cambridge, MA: Harvard UP, 1962.
Hunter, Lynette. *Rhetorical Stance in Modern Literature: Allegories of Love and Death*. New York: St. Martin's, 1984.
Isocrates. *Isocrates*. Ed. George Norlin. 3 Vols. Cambridge: Harvard UP, 1962.
Jones, John. *The Egotistical Sublime: A History of Wordsworth's Imagination*. London: Chatto & Windus, 1954.
Kennedy, George A. *Quintilian*. New York: Twayne Publishers, 1969.
Kimball, Bruce A. *Orators and Philosophers: A History of the Idea of Liberal Education*. New York: Columbia UP, 1986.
Kinneavy, James L. *A Theory of Discourse*. New York: W.W. Norton, 1971.
Kneale, J. Douglas. *Monumental Writing: Aspects of Rhetoric in Wordsworth's Poetry*. Lincoln: U of Nebraska P, 1988.
Kosko, Bart. *Fuzzy Thinking*. New York: Hyperion, 1993.
Kroeber, Karl. *Ecological Literary Criticism: Romantic Imagining and the Biology of Mind*. New York: Columbia UP, 1994.
Langbaum, Robert. *The Poetry of Experience*. New York: Random House, 1957.
Leader, Zachary. *Revision and Romantic Authorship*. Oxford: Clarendon, 1996.
Locke, John. *An Essay Concerning Human Understanding*. Oxford: Oxford UP, 1979.

Longinus. "On the Sublime." *Criticism: The Major Texts*. Ed. Walter Jackson Bate. New York: Harcourt Brace Jovanovich, 1970. 62–75.

Marrou, H. I. "Isocrates." *A History of Education in Antiquity*. Third ed. Trans. George Lamb. New York: Sheed and Ward, 1956. 79–94.

Nabholtz, John. *"My Reader, My Fellow Laborer": A Study of English Romantic Prose*. Columbia, MI: U of Missouri P, 1986.

———. "Romantic Prose and Classical Rhetoric." *Wordsworth Circle* 11 (1980): 119–26.

Neel, Jasper. *Plato, Derrida, and Writing*. Carbondale, IL: Southern Illinois UP, 1988.

Parrish, Stephen Maxfield. *The Art of the Lyrical Ballads*. Cambridge, MA: Harvard UP, 1973.

Peiffer, Barbara. "Godwinian Influences in Wordsworth's *The Borderers*: Reconciling Head and Heart." *Emporia State Research Studies* 37.1 (1988): 18–29.

Pfau, Thomas. "'Elementary Feelings' and 'Distorted Language': The Pragmatics of Culture in Wordsworth's Preface to Lyrical Ballads." *New Literary History* 24.1 (1993): 125–146.

Pirsig, Robert. *Zen and the Art of Motorcycle Maintenance*. New York: Bantam, 1974.

Plato. *Gorgias*. Trans. W. C. Helmbold. Bobbs-Merrill, 1952.

Pope, Alexander. *The Poems of Alexander Pope*. Ed. John Butt. New Haven: Yale UP, 1963.

Postman, Neil. *Amusing Ourselves to Death: Public Discourse in the Age of Show Business*. New York: Penguin, 1985.

Prigogine, Ilya and Isabelle Stengers. *Order Out of Chaos: Man's New Dialogue With Nature*. New York: Bantam, 1984.

Quintilian, Marcus Fabius. *Institutes of Oratory; or Education of an Orator*. 2 vols. Trans. John Selby Watson. London: George Bell & Sons, 1899.

Rader, Melvin. *Wordsworth: A Philosophical Approach*. Oxford: Clarendon, 1967.

Rajan, Tilottama. *The Supplement of Reading: Figures of Understanding in Romantic Theory and Practice*. New York: Cornell UP, 1990.

Rosenblatt, Louise. *The Reader, the Text, the Poem: The Transactional Theory of the Literary Work*. Carbondale, IL: Southern Illinois UP, 1978.

Rudy, John B. "Beyond Vocation and Ego: Self-displacement in Wordsworth's 1803 Memorials." *Studies in English Literature, 1500-1900* 29.4 (1989): 637–653.

———. *Wordsworth and the Zen Mind: the Poetry of Self-Emptying.* Albany, NY: State U of New York P, 1996.

Ruoff, Gene W. "Wordsworth on Language: Toward a Radical Poetics for English Romanticism." *Wordsworth Circle* 3 (1972): 204–11.

Rzepka, Charles J. *The Self as Mind: Vision and Identity in Wordsworth, Coleridge and Keats.* Cambridge, MA: Harvard UP, 1986.

Schapiro, Barbara. "Wordsworth and the Psychoanalytic Relational Model." *Mosaic* 25.1: 29–43.

Schumacher, E. F. *Small is Beautiful: Economics as if People Mattered.* New York: Harper and Row, 1973.

Sebberson, David. "Practical Reasoning, Rhetoric, and Wordsworth's 'Preface'." *Spirits of Fire: English Romantic Writers and Contemporary Historical Methods.* Rutherford, NJ: Fairleigh Dickinson UP, 1990. 95–111.

Sharrock, Roger. "Wordsworth on Science and Poetry." *Review of English Literature* 3.4 (1962): 42–50.

———. "Wordsworth's Revolt Against Literature." *Essays in Criticism* 3 (1953): 396–412.

Stallknecht, Newton P. *Strange Seas of Thought: Studies in William Wordsworth's Philosophy of Man and Nature.* Bloomington, IN: Indiana UP, 1958. Rpt of 1945 edition.

Stoddard, Eve Walsh. "*The Borderers*: A Critique of Both Reason and Feeling as Moral Agents." *Wordsworth Circle* 11 (1980): 93–97.

Terranella, Ronald L. *The Piagetian Epistemology of William Wordsworth: A Reconsideration of the Poet's Genius.* Lewiston: Edward Mellen, 1998.

Untersteiner, Mario. *The Sophists.* Trans. Kathleen Freeman. New York: Philosophical Library, 1954.

Williams, William Carlos. *Spring and All. Imaginations.* NY: New Directions, 1970. 88–151.

Wordsworth, William. *The Borderers.* Ed. Robert Osborn. New York: Cornell UP, 1982.

———. *Letters of William Wordsworth.* Ed. Alan G. Hill. New York: Oxford UP, 1984.

———. *Poetical Works*. Ed. Thomas Hutchinson and Ernest de Selincourt. New York: Oxford UP, 1969.
———. *The Pedlar, Tintern Abbey, The Two-Part Prelude*. Ed. Jonathan Wordsworth. New York: Cambridge UP, 1985.
———. *The Prelude 1799, 1805, 1850*. Ed. Jonathan Wordsworth, M. H. Abrams, and Stephen Gill. New York: W. W. Norton, 1979.
———. *The Prose Works of William Wordsworth*. Ed. W. J. B. Owen and Jane Worthington Smyser. 3 vols. Oxford: Clarendon, 1974.
Wordsworth, William and Dorothy. *The Letters of William and Dorothy Wordsworth: The Early Years 1787-1805*. 2nd ed. Ed. Ernest De Selincourt. Rev. Chester L. Shaver. Oxford: Clarendon, 1967.
Worthington, Jane. *Wordsworth's Reading of Roman Prose*. New Haven: Yale UP, 1946.
Zukav, Gary. *The Dancing Wu Li Masters*. New York: Bantam, 1979.

Index

Abrams, M. H.
  and "organic metaphor," 174
  Cartesian assumptions of, 3–4, 145, 185n. 2
  generalizations about Romanticism, 185n. 3
  mentioned, 6, 10, 89, 90, 187n. 2
aesthetics, 35–6
Aristotle
  mentioned, 15, 40
  model of knowledge, 16, 43, 76
  views of rhetoric, 20, 133, 181n. 3
Arnold, Matthew
  mentioned, 20, 32
  view of education, 170–72
  view of Wordsworth's "philosophy," 2, 4, 166, 179n. 3
  view of Wordsworth's use of "nature," 92

Bate, Jonathan, 6, 179, 184n. 3
Bateson, Gregory
  acknowledgement of, xii
  concepts of calibration and feedback, 113–17, 145
  concept of "ecology of mind," 10, 81, 174, 184n. 3
  concept of "map containment," 91, 103, 185n. 1
  mentioned, 7, 23, 142, 164, 183n. 1
  view of epistemology, 73, 85, 87
  view of limits of reason, 173
  view of mental process, 101, 105–07, 109–11, 135, 180n. 6
Berman, Morris
  acknowledgement of, xii
  concept of "Cartesian paradigm," 42–5
  concept of "participating" and "nonparticipating" consciousness, 53–4, 96
  mentioned, 12, 51, 85
  view of "scientific epistemology," 9, 29, 91, 172, 181n. 1
Bialostosky, Don H., 34, 76, 182n. 6
Bohm, David
  mentioned, 88
  view of art as a way of knowing, 143, 169
  view of fluid nature of "reality," 51, 85, 104, 135, 182n. 2
  view of language, 1, 179n. 1
Bohr, Niels, 31
Burke, Edmund, 9, 25, 55, 180n. 11
Burke, Kenneth
  concept of "identification," 145–46, 150–52
  mentioned, 23
  moral vision, 167, 171, 173
  view of rhetoric, 24, 118, 122, 138
Bush, Douglas, 68

calibration, 113–16, 137, 145, 147
  See also Bateson, Gregory
Cartesian
  assumptions, 3, 5–7
  dichotomies, 1, 4
  "filter," 2
  model of knowledge, 1, 8, 29, 42–3, 167–71

See also Descartes, René
Chandler, James K., 89, 91, 182n. 5
Clarke, C. C., 2, 94, 147
Coleridge, Samuel Taylor
  concept of imagination, 67, 107
  intellectual differences with
    Wordsworth, 32–4, 67, 99, 139,
    174, 182n. 4, 182n. 5
  mentioned, 4, 89, 125, 186n. 3,
    187n. 9
composition
  and habits of mind, 125
  and knowing, 10–11, 18, 46, 126,
    168
  and rhetorical stance, 145
  and Wordsworth's "literary theory,"
    123, 125, 134–35, 137–38, 141
  as field of study, 8, 38, 43, 137
  Quintilian's views of, 118, 125–26,
    129–31
consciousness
  and mindful pattern in nature, 1, 51,
    111, 180n. 6
  and perception, 96
  non-participating, 41–4, 54
  participating, 43–4, 85, 93, 160–61
  religious, 69
  Wordsworth's concept of "two
    consciousnesses," 7, 91–3
context
  and doxa, 21
  and kairos, 17, 22, 115, 117, 151
  and interpretation, 16, 18, 31,
    73, 170, 175
  and moral judgment, 41, 43
  and "systematic thinking," 80, 167
  different levels of, 107, 170
  of this text, 10, 12, 16, 18, 23

role in calibration and feedback,
  114–18
continuum
  in epistemology, 10, 77, 159,
    180n. 6
  in the rhetorical tradition, 8, 15
  of modes of perception, 96
  of perception and reflection in
    Wordsworth's poetry, 144, 153
  opposed to dichotomy, 5, 66, 135
Creatura
  Jung's concept of, 109, 180n. 6
  See also Pleroma
cybernetics
  and complexity, 176,
  and systems thinking, 7, 107, 109,
    117, 135

Damasio, Antonio, 7, 117, 133–34,
  180n. 7, 183n. 1, 186n. 7
Danford, John W., 45
Darling, David, 88
Descartes, René
  and non-participating
    consciousness, 53–4
  influence on literary criticism, 5–6
  mentioned, 43, 87, 105, 127, 174
  See also Cartesian
dialectic
  and the tuning of relationships, 60
  between logos and kairos, 121
  in "We are Seven," 156–57
  Platonic, 16, 22, 37–8, 182–83n. 7
  relation to rhetoric (in Aristotle), 20,
    181n. 3
dichotomy, 98–9, 109, 133, 160
  See also continuum
difference

and cybernetics, 135
and mental process, 109–11, 185n. 1
and poetic meaning, 154–55
Bateson's concept of, 109–11
"difference that makes a difference," 162, 177
Wordsworth's concept of, 65, 110–11, 113
disenchantment, 53–4
doxa, 20–2, 28, 43, 117
   See also context, kairos, logos
dualism, 7, 42, 87, 92, 106–07, 143
   See also Descartes, René
Durrant, Geoffrey, 2, 61–2, 182n. 3

ecology
   and systems thinking, 8
   as context for understanding Wordsworth, 1
   as framing concept for inquiry, 174–77
   of mind, Bateson, 10
   of mind, Wordsworth, 65–6, 81–2, 101–06, 115
   of mind, in "Tintern Abbey," 157–60
Einstein, Albert, 31, 36
emergence, 37, 108, 109, 185
empiricism
   and rationalism, 43
   as an approach to knowing, 26, 43,\ 53
   dilemma associated with, 87–8
   Wordsworth's commitment to, 68–71, 98
Engell, James, 67
epistemology
   and "map containment," 91
   cultural, in Edmund Burke, 9
   scientific, 9–10, 54–5, 92, 105, 174
   reason-centered, 25–6, 54–5
   rhetorical, 73–81, 157, 166
   Wordsworth's 5, 10–11, 24, 115, 179n. 2
experience
   and logos, 78–80
   experience-centered model of knowing, 21, 23, 27
   importance for Isocrates, 40
   Langbaum's "doctrine of experience," 4–5
   poetry and, 28, 76–7
   power of personal experience, 75
   See also empiricism, nature, second nature
experiment
   this text as an experiment, xi
   Wordsworth's epistemic experiments, 24, 55, 169, 179

feedback, 113–15, 137
   See also Bateson, Gregory
French revolution,
   and limits of reason, 25–6, 55, 58, 127
   mentioned, 9, 60, 180n. 11
Frost, Robert, 46

Garber, Frederick, 2
Gilligan, Carol, 41–2
Grob, Alan, 2, 182n. 3

habits
   of expression, 36
   of thinking and knowing, 42, 77
   related to cultural traditions, 55, 94

habits of mind
   and Quintilian's "habits of meditation," 129–32
   importance in mental process, 11, 23, 78–82, 101, 106–08, 115, 123, 125–29, 143, 175

Hairston, Maxine, 38
Hartley, David, 35, 66, 129, 182
Hartman, Geoffrey, 56
Hayden, John O., 104, 182n. 4, 185n. 3
Heisenberg, Werner, 31
Hewitt, Regina, 6, 20, 61, 88, 146, 179n. 4, 181n. 4
Hoopes, Robert, 58, 180n. 12
Hume, David, 9, 45, 53, 118, 188
Hunter, Lynette, 121, 145

identification
   and "natural language," 94
   and sympathy, 60, 152–53
   and pleasure, 152–53
   as a poetic device, 137
   in "Tintern Abbey," 158–62
   in "We are Seven," 154–57
   Kenneth Burke's concept of, 145–46, 150–52

imagination
   and rhetorical engagement with an audience, 125, 128, 137, 140–41
   and logos, 168, 175
   as point of connection between body and mind, 27, 66–8, 81, 105, 107, 162
   differences between Coleridge's and Wordsworth's view of, 105, 107
   in critical responses to Wordsworth, 3, 56, 60, 182
   limits on, 137–38
   mentioned, 41, 51, 65, 70, 78, 162, 183n. 3
   related to reason, 27, 66–68

intuition, 22, 43, 137
invitation, 141, 163, 164

Isocrates
   and rhetorical tradition of thinking, 23, 39–41, 122
   as opponent of Plato, 16, 39–41, 115, 117
   mentioned, 15, 28, 186n. 4

Jones, John, 2

kairos
   and limits of rational systems, 22
   and moral judgment, 41, 115, 168
   and rhetorical tradition, 22–3, 122, 151
   and truth, 117
   defined, 17
   related to logos, 22, 28, 121, 128–29, 151, 168, 176

Kennedy, George A., 125, 129
Kinneavy, James L., 145, 187n. 1
Kosko, Bart, 29
Kroeber, Karl, 2, 6, 179n. 4

Langbaum, Robert, 4–5
"larger processes," 60–1, 70, 81, 142, 173–75
Leader, Zachary, 7, 18
literary criticism, xii, 1–2, 133
Locke, John
   influence on Wordsworth, 35
   mentioned, 43, 53
   views on language, perception and "objective reality," 8, 118, 180n.

Index

9, 184n. 1
views on misguided reasoning,
   183n. 3
logos
   and meaning-making, 28, 46–7,
      118, 168, 175–77
   and moral choice, 42, 168, 175–77
   and personal assumptions, 78, 175–77
   definitions of, 22, 67, 118
   logos-centered model of knowing,
      28, 41–2, 168, 175–77
   relationship with kairos, 121–22,
      129, 151, 175–77
   rhetorical appeal to, 151
   See also context, doxa, kairos
Longinus, 23, 150–51

meaning-making
   and logos, 177
   and poesis, 163
   and rhetoric, 119–20, 126
   as central quality of human beings,
      28, 166, 186n. 7
   role of feeling in, 79, 186n. 7
mental processes
   and "associationism," 87, 107
   and poetry, 144–45, 154, 157–58,
      162–63
   Bateson's views of, 109–11, 185n. 1
   continuum of, 8, 101, 106, 174,
      186n. 7
   Wordsworth's interest in, 10, 21, 92,
      174
   related to biology, 66–7, 101, 106,
      109
Mittelstaedt, Horst, 113

Nabholtz, John, 77, 124–25, 181n. 7,
   185–86n. 3, 186n. 5
nature
   as central concept in Wordsworth's
      poetry, 24, 26–7, 57–69, 113,
      128, 135–37
   as larger mindlike process, 10, 88,
      117, 174
   difference between Pope's "Nature"
      and Wordsworth's, 119
   in Gorgias, 22
   in "Tintern Abbey," 158–62
   interface with human beings, 1, 109,
      143
   opposed to "second nature," 89, 91–7, 138
   See also second nature
Neel, Jasper, 31, 37–9
non-linear, 65, 109

objective
   knowledge, 10, 54–5, 100, 167–68
   opposed to rhetorical, 119–20
   opposed to subjective, 87, 92, 119–20
   thinking, 2, 105
   See also subjective
objectivity
   and moral choices, 42
   as stance taken toward reality, 171–75
   See also subjectivity

pantheism, 111
paradigm, 7, 29, 38, 43
"pattern which connects," 158, 162,
   164

perception
- and "feeling," 3, 77–82, 135–36
- and moral action, 42, 184n. 1
- and "reality," 8
- and rhetorical tradition, 22, 26, 34, 42
- and subjectivity, 87, 181n. 6
- as base of knowledge, xii, 4–5, 10–11, 137–38
- as central feature of Wordsworth's epistemology, 21, 26–7, 67–9, 76–82, 87–115
- as problem in philosophy, 45, 53
- devalued by Cartesian model of knowing, 42–3
- in Wordsworth's poetry, 145, 148, 157, 162, 164, 166, 168, 176, 180n. 8

Pfau, Thomas, 92

philosophy
- and models of knowing, 71, 117–19
- as "higher knowledge," 117–19
- as mode of discourse, 24
- critical views of Wordsworth's, 2, 4, 20–1, 32, 35, 166, 179n. 3, 182n. 3, 183n. 9
- emerging from rhetoric, 20, 121–22
- empirical, 16
- Isocratean views of, 41
- mechanical, 53, 114
- moral, 9, 74, 98, 128
- opposed to rhetoric, 8, 10,
- Platonic, 115,
- Wordsworth's, 146, 149

Piaget, Jean, 41, 179n. 2

Pirsig, Robert, 15, 27, 29

Plato
- battle with Sophists, 117
- bid for discursive power, 31, 37–9
- domination of modern thinking, 22, 42–3, 181n. 1
- ideas compared to those of Isocrates, 15–16, 40–1, 183n. 8
- views on rhetoric and dialectic, 22–3, 119, 122, 182–83n. 7

pleasure
- and knowledge, xi, 11, 69, 139, 148
- and engagement, 138, 141, 148
- and rhetoric, 152, 183n. 4
- dualistic definitions of, 93, 97, 121, 166
- in the Preface to *Lyrical Ballads*, xi, 11, 36, 69

Pleroma
- Jung's concept of, 109, 179–80n. 6
- *See also* Creatura

poesis, 11, 28, 104, 163

Pope, Alexander, 9, 119–20

praxis, 40, 82, 169

"pre-established codes of decision," 1, 90–1, 96–9, 100, 128, 136, 175

purpose
- and reason, 54–5, 96, 173
- and rhetoric, 24, 118, 122, 133, 146
- in composition, 46, 125–28
- of poetry, 7, 33, 35, 94, 125–28, 149
- Wordsworth's moral and social, 4, 12, 15, 19, 88, 135

quantum physics, 31, 43, 176

Quintilian
- and rhetorical tradition, 23–4, 115, 177, 186n. 4
- relation of central concepts to Wordsworth, 15–16, 118, 123–41, 160, 186n. 7

stress on composing, 7, 27–8, 118
Wordsworth's knowledge of, 10

Rader, Melvin, 2, 182n. 3
Rajan, Tilottama, 5–6
rationalism, 43
   See also empiricism
reason
   and habits of mind, 126–28, 180n. 11
   and logos, 118
   and rhetorical appeals, 79–81, 118, 123, 125, 183n. 4
   "circular," compared with feedback loops, 135
   connected with emotion or "feeling," 8, 133, 186n. 7
   instrumental, 9, 55–6, 167–71
   limits of reason-centered epistemology, 25–7, 53–6, 167–71, 180n. 11, 183n. 3
   related to perception, 105, 137–38
   Right Reason, 9, 56, 58, 66, 180n. 12
   Wordsworth's position toward, 25–7, 56–60
recursive
   approach of this text, 25
   model of mental process, 101–07, 135, 137, 176
   nature of social change, 127
   processes of knowing,
      in general, xv, 24–7
      in "Tintern Abbey," 65–7
   relationship among modes of discourse, 24
      See also cybernetics
representation

and reality, 10–11
and rhetoric, 117, 121, 138
biological and linguistic, 108, 186n. 7
centrality in rhetorical epistemology, 78–82, 88, 105
importance in mental process, 78–82, 109, 186n. 7
poetry as medium of, 149
Rosenblatt, Louise, 95–6
Rudy, John, 7, 60–1, 70
Rzepka, Charles, 2, 71

Schumacher, E. F., 171
Sebberson, David, 41, 53, 115, 183n. 9, 185n. 1
second nature
   and cultural norms, 127–28, 138
   defined, 89–94
   opposed to "nature," 89–94, 138, 160
   See also nature
Sharrock, Roger, 4
similitude, 110, 113
Socrates, 22, 38, 119
Stallknecht, Newton P., 2
subjective
   basis of epistemology, 87
   critical description of Wordsworth, 4–5, 180n. 8
   opposed to objective, 121, 167–71
   See also objective
subjectivity
   Wordsworth's poetics of, 4–6
   See also objectivity
succedaneum, 89
systemic, 7, 18, 107, 109, 117
systems thinking, 8, 107, 185n. 3

teacher
  nature as, 98, 138
  role in the dance of knowing, 37–8
  Wordsworth's aim to be, 20
teaching, 37–8
tuning, 27, 60, 114–15, 129

uncertainty, 31

value
  and meaning, 18, 44, 78–9, 105, 117, 146
  and moral judgment, 45, 60, 146
  and pleasure, 138
  and poetry, 143–44, 146, 159–63, 168
  as central to knowing, 9–10, 167–75
  divorced from "fact" and "truth," 9–10, 53–4
  importance of assumptions about, 31

Wordsworth, William
  works
    Borderers, The, xiii, 56–7, 70, 183n. 4
    "Essay on Morals," xiii, 17–18, 23, 46, 71, 73, 79–80, 82, 92–3, 94, 100, 103, 118, 127
    "Expostulation and Reply," 97, 98, 99
    Lyrical Ballads, xi, xiii, 1, 3–6, 16, 18, 33–4, 46, 68, 74, 82, 95, 98, 103, 117, 125, 127, 131–32, 135, 139, 140, 144, 147, 149, 169, 181–84, 186, 188, 190–91
    Pedlar, The, xiii, 111–13, 157–63, 192
    Preface to *Lyrical Ballads*, 1800, xiii, 3, 33, 36, 110, 149
    Preface to *Lyrical Ballads*, 1802, xi, xiii, 19, 36, 93, 103, 169
    Prelude, 1805, xiii, 18, 56–60, 62–63, 65–67, 89, 108, 183
    Prelude, 1850, xiii, 18, 57, 59, 60, 63, 89–90, 108, 112
    "Solitary Reaper, The," viii, 154, 163, 166, 168
    "Tables Turned, The," 97–98
    "Tintern Abbey," viii, xiii, 7, 21, 67, 91, 154, 157, 161, 163, 192
    "We are Seven," viii, 153–154, 157
Worthington, Jane, 124–25, 185n. 3

Studies in Nineteenth-Century British Literature

Regina Hewitt, General Editor

Books in this series examine the poetry and prose produced by British writers from the time of the French Revolution to the death of Queen Victoria. Historical events—rather than traditional literary categories or dates—define the scope of the series because they better convey a sense of the social consciousness that animates literary undertakings during this age. While the series includes a wide range of approaches to nineteenth-century British works, its special focus is on studies that relate this literature to its cultural context(s). Manuscripts addressing their subjects' social, political, or historical situations, ideals, influences, or receptions are especially welcome; manuscripts analyzing the implications of classifying this literature as "Romantic" or "Victorian" or of separating it into genres are also encouraged. Authors should write in English, though they may appropriately compare British works with those in other languages.

Authors wishing to have works considered for this series should contact:

Regina Hewitt
c/o Dr. Heidi Burns
Peter Lang Publishing, Inc.
516 N. Charles St., 2nd Floor
Baltimore, MD 21201

To order other books in this series, please contact our Customer Service Department:

(800) 770-LANG (within the U.S.)
(212) 647-7706 (outside the U.S.)
(212) 647-7707 FAX

Or browse online by series at:

www.peterlang.com

OHIO UNIVERSITY LIBRARY

Please return this book as soon as you have finished with it. In order to avoid a fine it must be returned by the latest date stamped below. All books are subject to recall after two weeks or immediately if needed for reserve.

CF